Asymmetrical Warfare

D0030037

ISSUES IN TWENTY-FIRST-CENTURY WARFARE

SERIES EDITORS

Capt. Roger W. Barnett, USN (Ret.), Ph.D.
Naval War College

Stephen J. Cimbala, Ph.D.
Penn State University

ADVISORY BOARD

Col. C. Kenneth Allard, USA (Ret.), Ph.D.
Potomac Strategies International, LLC

Capt. John P. Cann, USNR (Ret.), Ph.D.
U.S. Marine Corps Command and Staff College

Colin Gray, D. Phil.
Centre for Strategic Studies, University of Reading

Benjamin S. Lambeth, Ph.D.
RAND

Mark D. Mandeles, Ph.D.
The J. de Bloch Group

Michael F. Paukovic, Ph.D.
Hawaii Pacific University

Capt. Peter M. Swartz, USN (Ret.)
CNA Corporation

Asymmetrical Warfare

*Today's Challenge to U.S.
Military Power*

ROGER W. BARNETT

BRASSEY'S, INC.
Washington, D.C.

Copyright (c) 2003 by Brassey's, Inc.

Published in the United States by Brassey's, Inc. All rights reserved. No part of this book may be reproduced in any manner whatsoever without written permission from the publisher, except in the case of brief quotations embodied in critical articles and reviews.

Library of Congress Cataloging-in-Publication Data

Barnett, Roger W.
  Asymmetrical warfare : today's challenge to U.S. military power /
Roger W. Barnett.—1st ed.
      p. cm.
Includes bibliographical references and index.
   ISBN 1-57488-562-6 (hardcover)—ISBN 1-57488-563-4 (paperback)
   1. United States—Military policy. 2. Asymmetric warfare. 3. World
politics—21st century. I. Title.
   UA23 .B3357 2003
   355'.033573—dc21
                                    2002008008

Printed in the United States of America on acid-free paper that meets the American National Standards Institute Z39-48 Standard.

Brassey's, Inc.
22841 Quicksilver Drive
Dulles, Virginia 20166

First Edition

10 9 8 7 6 5 4 3 2 1

To Sandy

Contents

Introduction

[W]hen a nation state or national armed force, (which adheres to certain rules and will only use limited force to obtain a limited goal), faces off with one of these types of organizations [the Japanese Aum Shinrikyo cult; and . . . terrorist groups like Osama bin Ladin's] (which never observe any rules and which are not afraid to fight an unlimited war using unlimited means), it will often prove very difficult for the nation state or national armed force to gain the upper hand.

Qiao Liang and Wang Xiangsui, Unrestricted Warfare

Since the Second World War, various official and nonofficial statements have called into question whether, given the nature of modern war, even the just cause of defense can legitimize resort to armed force.

James Turner Johnson

What if they gave a war and nobody came? This, of course, has been a goal of many who have witnessed the horrors and consequences of war and of many who have not. Indeed, in 1928 fifteen states signed an international treaty for the purpose of outlawing war. Named the Pact of Paris, or the Kellogg-Briand Treaty, it became effective on July 24, 1929, having been ratified by the United States, Great Britain, France, Poland, Czechoslovakia, and Belgium—as well as the future Axis Powers of World War II: Italy, Japan, and Germany. Ultimately, forty states acceded to the treaty, which in Article I stated: "The High Contracting Parties solemnly declare in the names of their respective peoples that they condemn recourse to war for the solution of international controversies, and renounce it as an instrument of national policy in their relations with one another."[1] Noble though the cause, the treaty was tragically ineffective, for the ravages of World War II followed in only a dozen

---

[1] John Norton Moore, Guy B. Roberts, and Robert F. Turner, *National Security Law Documents* (Durham, N.C.: Carolina Academic Press, 1995), 140.

years. One might observe that the ratifiers listed above—with the note-worthy exception of the United States—became the roll call of those most grievously affected by the war.

Whether conflict is prompted by the ambitions of aggressor states, irreconcilable territorial disputes, historical grievances, or ideological incompatibilities, its resolution can employ only a few tools. In the absence of an overarching international authority with the power to make and enforce decisions about interstate issues, each state must rely on the instruments available to it. There are essentially only three: diplomacy, economic actions, and the use of military force. Obviously, the first is preferable. If words don't work, sometimes money does. But, ultimately, the use of force might have to be resorted to in order to redress grievances or settle disputes.

Unquestionably, diplomacy in all its variants can deal with some con-tentious issues. Diplomacy requires at least two parties with a willingness—for whatever reason—to settle the issues involved, a condition often lack-ing in disputes. Economic sanctions have a checkered history, but stand as the bridging measure between, as Winston Churchill remarked in the aftermath of the Korean War: "Jaw, jaw," and "war, war." Evidence appears to be growing, however, that economic sanctions might cause even more damage and pain than the use of violent force: "The irony is that in con-trast to the others, this device—economic sanctions—is deployed fre-quently, by large states rather than small ones, and may have contributed to more deaths during the post-Cold War era than all weapons of mass destruction throughout history."[2]

Generally speaking, if diplomacy doesn't work, if economic actions such as sanctions are ineffective or not employed because of their poten-tial consequences, or if those approaches are irrelevant to the problem at hand, then one is left with the prospect of either threatening or using force. One pivotal issue involves the transition from one form of conflict resolution to another. When does one decide, or how does one determine that diplomacy and other forms of peaceful mediation have been inef-fective and that other measures are warranted? This is a matter of art, not science. Inevitably, some will be convinced that force should never be employed, that one should always "Give peace another chance."

---

[2]John Mueller and Karl Mueller, "Sanctions of Mass Destruction," *Foreign Affairs*, May/June 1999, 49–53 [electronic version].

Paradoxes abound. In the first place, if diplomacy and economics are ineffective, one must possess the means and the will to use force if that road is to be chosen. Both are necessary, for the absence of one or the other spells impotence.

This raises the subject of deterrence: the threat either to proceed in such a fashion that an aggressor, or perpetrator, will be worse off after having acted than before, or to prevent any action on the part of the perpetrator from succeeding. The former is called deterrence by the threat of retaliation, the effects of which would be unacceptable to the recipient of the retaliation; the latter, deterrence by denial—the prospective perpetrator assesses that it cannot accomplish its objectives, and therefore elects not to try. Some actions are not deterrable, such as those undertaken by irrational actors—those who either cannot perform the cost/benefit calculus or are willing to act contrary to their own value system—or those undertaken for the sole purpose of inflicting pain, irrespective of the consequences. The September 2001 attacks on the United States were no doubt undeterrable for either, or perhaps both, of these reasons. A deterrent threat, in any event, requires that the deterrer both maintain a relevant capability and also a perceived credibility to employ that capability. It is the product of capability and will that deters by threat of retaliation. This "product" is the source of the paradox, well known even to the Romans: *si vis pacem, para bellum* (If you seek peace, prepare for war).

Because it is the product of capability and will that deters in the case of retaliation, if either become small, the deterrent effect is greatly diminished. While policy ambiguity might be useful politically, it works diametrically against the ability to deter. If a state articulates a clear policy that incursions against its territorial integrity will be met with a very powerful military response, the deterrent effect is stronger than if it makes the pronouncement "Aggressors will be made to regret their actions." Ambiguity can be useful in such situations, but only to amplify the deterrent effect, not to establish it. Thus, "Aggressors will be met with overwhelming military force, and the use of nuclear weapons cannot be ruled out," offers a strong deterrent threat reinforced by the ambiguity of just what form the military hammer will take. One of the major difficulties in deterrence by threat of retaliation is the selection of suitable targets. If for one or another reason, targets are ruled out, then deterrence is undermined.

Deterrence by denial, the second form of deterrence, is more difficult both to understand and to analyze. It seeks to deal with those kinds of encroachments against which deterrence by threat of punishment is ineffective. Terrorism is the prime example of an activity that requires deterrence by denial. It says to prospective terrorists, "You may be able to harm me—even to give me great pain—but whatever it is you want, I will not let you have it." This is the basis of the policy of not negotiating with hostage takers, for example. It requires courage, tenacity, and the perceptions of those qualities by potential actors. Having a track record for not giving in to threats helps as well. Of course, ambiguity has no place here; in fact, it would be counterproductive.

Deterrence is a complex subject, but one thing well understood about deterrence in both its forms is that it fails. Why should it fail? The range of answers narrows to:

- The defender's retaliatory capability was not credible to the attacker, or was not deemed relevant to the issue;

- The will on the part of the defender to use available capability effectively was not perceived as sufficient;

- The attacker believed that success would result, because of the impress of some asymmetrical capability, even in the face of a resolute, capable defender;

- The attack was irrational—no rational actor would have calculated that it would have succeeded; or

- The attack was not deterrable in the first place. Actions that seek merely to inflict pain, or that are taken out of vengeance, for example, tend not to be deterrable.

In order to deter successfully, the capability to carry out threats to use military force—either in retaliation or preemptively—must be credible, and the will to carry out such threats must be manifest. The greater the defender's combination of capability and will, the less likely the perpetrator will be to believe he can prevail nonetheless. And still, deterrence can fail because of error, asymmetry, irrationality, or irrelevance. If deterrence fails, the central issue then becomes how most efficiently and effectively to use the military instrument in order to prevail—or, at a minimum, not to lose.

Or, perhaps, the use of force might even be rendered moot by the failure of deterrence. Conceivably, if deterrence were to fail, one might choose not to use force because the results could not be foreseen or because the entire range of potential outcomes appears unfavorable. This would seem to place the deterrent threat in the form of a called bluff, but the situation is far richer. For example, imagine that a powerful, very hostile government were to seize power in Russia. It then issues a threat to conduct a single nuclear missile attack against a population target in the United States unless the United States establishes a line of credit of $500 billion "in compensation for past crimes against the Russian people." Clearly, the U.S. deterrent threat would entail not meeting such an extortionate threat and promising to retaliate against any attack on the U.S. homeland in such measure that the attacker could not profit and would dearly regret it. U.S. policy makers who issue such a threat would be earnest in so doing; that is, in their minds, no bluff would be involved. But what if deterrence were to fail in this case? The United States would suffer great damage from the detonation of a nuclear weapon on its territory. If it were to retaliate, however, would it not greatly risk evoking even greater response from the remaining weapons in the Russian arsenal? Could the United States tolerate such an escalatory chain of events? Is it rational to attempt to determine which side in this instance has a higher threshold of pain? Clearly, the answers are "yes," "no," and "no." One must conclude, therefore, that in such an instance, if deterrence were to fail, the United States would necessarily lose.

Conceivably, the United States could be the victim of the nuclear strike and still be forced to pay the extortion. Retaliation would not only be exclusively for the purpose of vengeance, but it would also cause greater, no doubt unacceptable, damage in response from the other side. Here, by fear of the ultimate consequences, the United States would have been checkmated. Facing such a prospect, and in the absence of an effective ballistic missile defense against such an attack, the United States must pay the extortionate sum. No doubt it would have to continue to pay until it found some other way to respond and relieve the danger. This describes the extraordinary case where deterrence would be trumped by the catastrophic prospect of its failure. No adequate response could be mounted that would offset the prospective losses. The United States could not tolerate the failure of deterrence in this instance; if deterrence were to fail, the United States would lose, and the loss would be of the greatest significance.

The benefit to be gained by a ballistic missile defense in this scenario would be to raise the uncertainty of the success of a small attack, thereby facing the prospective attacker with a choice of the failure of a small attack or launching a much larger strike, which would incur the highest of risks. Some might argue, on the other hand, that a ballistic missile defense would make no difference in this scenario, because the threat could be substantiated instead with smuggled suitcase bombs, against which a ballistic missile defense would be totally ineffective. While true, this argument is irrelevant. It is no valid criticism of penicillin that it does not cure the common cold. Penicillin provided revolutionary relief against bacterial infection; viruses must be dealt with by other means. This in no way diminishes the need for, or the value of, penicillin. The same is true with ballistic missile defenses and suitcase bombs. It is no valid criticism of ballistic missile defenses to argue that they do not cure suitcase bombs. In such an instance, one must necessarily deal with both, but the debating ground should shift to priorities and costs. The existence of a ballistic missile defense can make a great difference in this case, however, by altering the strategic calculus. A defense, which the prospective attacker must assume will be effective, changes the ante in the contest. It means that if the attacker is required to actually fire missiles, enough must be sent to overwhelm the defense. This, materially, would affect both the probability and the size of a response in kind.

Deterrence, it should be noted, is wholly defensive. It seeks to forestall actions by an adversary that one would find undesirable or worse. One problem with deterrence is that it is not directly observable. That an adversary does not attack or act in contrary ways does not mean that it is deterred; after all, it might harbor no such intentions. All that can be said is that a particular situation is *consistent with deterrence working*. It is impossible, of course, to prove the negative—to determine conclusively why some event did *not* take place.

It is a curious paradox that deterrence can be based either on strength or on weakness. Based on strength, deterrence threatens to produce effects that are unacceptable to the perpetrator. Based on weakness, it promises something different—perhaps chaos, an automatic retort, or the unleashing of uncontrollable forces. In the latter case, the deterrer, in effect, says, "I am weak. I am so weak that I have no other means to try to prevent your undesired acts." The Strangelovian "Doomsday

Machine," in which emplaced nuclear charges would explode automatically if a nuclear detonation were detected, offers an example in this category. Another example is placing strategic weapons on hair-triggers, a process called "launch on warning," or "launch under attack." This is a strategy of weakness, for it says to the opponent, "I am so weak that I cannot confidently ride out a first strike by you and still have sufficient forces to counterattack. Therefore, I must counterthrust as rapidly as I can on warning that you are about to attack, or on confirmation that an attack is in progress."

The nastier and the less ambiguous the deterrent threat—backed up by requisite capability—presumably, the higher the level of deterrence. Yet, a threat by the United States to bombard Mexico City with nuclear warheads in order to deter Mexicans from emigrating to the United States would clearly be excessive and, therefore, not credible. Likewise, the United States would not build a 60-megaton cobalt bomb[3] to deter long-range nuclear attack. By posing an apocalyptic response, such a bomb might act as a powerful deterrent, but it raises credibility questions as to whether it would be used if the bluff were called. A provocative, but academic and open, question involves whether such a horrific deterrent would lessen the prospect of the extortionate threat outlined above or whether it would be deemed incredible. Thus, if the military instrument must be used, it should be reliable and stand a good chance of securing victory—or the attainment of objectives. A fit is required between the quality of the threatened action and the deterrent threat, and the fit is tailored by constraining the deterrent so that it is credible. Tailoring involves issues of propriety and proportionality.

Deterrence is not the *objective* of policy. An objective might be "no violent use of force"—that policy goals should be pursued in a peaceful manner.[4] Deterrence, in contrast, is a *way*, or a *strategy*, to attain an objective of "no use of force." One does not value deterrence for itself, but for what it can accomplish.

---

[3]A cobalt bomb was a hypothetical nuclear weapon into which would be placed an amount of cobalt 59. The cobalt would be irradiated by the explosion of the nuclear core and create large amounts of toxic cobalt 60 (radioactive) fallout. It was conceived as, perhaps, the ultimate in a "dirty" nuclear weapon.

[4]Hereafter, the term "use of force" should be understood to mean that it is accompanied by acts of violence. Threats, for example, do not qualify as use of force.

Likewise, *stability* cannot be an objective of policy. However ano-dyne it sounds—who could favor instability?—the "pursuit of stability" is a fool's quest. "Stability" is a sterile political term that has no useful meaning or integrity outside a specific political setting. To say that a particular policy or effort is "destabilizing" has no meaning beyond "I don't like it."[5]

Change will take place in the international environment: states will rise, states will fall, states will experience internal turmoil, and states will alter course. Accordingly, a central question is not how stability is to be preserved, but how change can be accommodated—whether peacefully or violently. Although many of the world's states, including some of the largest and most successful, have become satisfied defenders of the status quo—and many equate a nonviolent status quo with stability—a classic analyst of international affairs cautioned years ago that "the defense of the status quo is not a policy which can be lastingly successful. It will end in war as surely as rigid conservatism will end in revolution. . . . To establish methods of peaceful change is therefore the fundamental prob-lem of international morality and of international politics."[6] While change is mandated, however, *peaceful change* cannot be foreordained.[7]

Foreseeably, then, the employment of force to attain objectives will retain value—whether to sovereign states, terrorists, extortionists, insur-

---

[5]Cf.: "Preserving regional stability. Often invoked, this goal is particularly imprecise, probably unat-tainable, and at odds with future trends. Major political and social change in the Gulf in the not too distant future is a certainty and will, by definition, be destabilizing. . . . The only realistic U.S. security objective in the Gulf is prevention of cross-border aggression." Graham E. Fuller and Ian O. Lesser, "Persian Gulf Myths," *Foreign Affairs*, May/June 1997, 44. Michael Ledeen argues, "When-ever I hear policy-makers talk about the wonders of 'stability,' I get the heebie-jeebies. . . . We are not going to fight foreign wars or send our money overseas merely to defend the status quo; we must have a suitably glorious objective." "American Power—For What: A Symposium," *Commentary*, January 2000 [Current News Supplement, January 5, 2000]. U.S. Deputy Secretary of Defense John Hamre might have prompted Ledeen's insight, as he lamented: "It worries me frankly that creating stability, political stability, is not a sufficiently justifiable reason to go to war. Instead, you have to find some transcendent reason that justifies or moves democracies to act." "Is Rationale for Waging War Changing?" *Defense Information and Electronics Report*, September 3, 1999, 21.

[6]Edward Hallett Carr, *The Twenty Years' Crisis, 1919–1939* (New York: Harper & Row, Publishers, Harper Torchbooks, 1939), 222.

[7]In this regard, Osgood and Tucker contend that "One simply cannot comprehend the rise, spread, and decline of ancient civilizations and peoples, or the creation, unification, expansion, and pro-tection of modern nation-states except in relation to force." Robert E. Osgood and Robert W. Tucker, *Force, Order, and Justice* (Baltimore, Md.: The Johns Hopkins University Press, 1967), 5.

gents, revolutionaries, or lunatics. The threat of the use of force can also have a key role to play in deterrence. Thus, organizations will undoubtedly maintain the capacity to employ force—either to actively pursue their objectives, or to defend against the attempts of others.

If an overarching objective is to ensure that change is wrought through peaceful means, however, then the use of force to secure or prevent change must be discouraged, or, at a minimum, severely restrained. Kellogg-Briand was merely one in a long series of efforts to prohibit the use of force in the resolution of conflict over change. Failing outright prohibition, efforts have centered on constraints. Telford Taylor notes, "Since the early civilizations men have speculated about ways of eliminating war, and since the Middle Ages one of those ways has been the enunciation of rules of conduct, which gradually assumed the characteristics of law."[8] This gives rise to a new set of concerns having to do with the morality, fairness, civility, consequences, and control of the use of force.

The trend line, Kellogg-Briand representing one point on that line, is both paradoxical and unmistakable:

> The late twentieth century has increasingly come to declare *all* war evil. . . . [P]eace is considered the natural state of relations . . . in which some degree of moral guilt is freely assessed equally both to those who kill to advance evil and those who kill to end it, to those who are aggressive and to those who resist aggrandizement.[9]

In this framework, not only is a resort to the use of force considered immoral, *how* the force is applied must be a first order consideration. This line of thought leads to questions of how much force must be applied; what kinds of force are politically, legally, and morally tolerable; and what should be put at risk in the application of force. Central to such issues is the determination of whether the use of military force stems from necessary or vital issues or from discretionary or optional considerations.

---

[8]Telford Taylor, "Just and Unjust Wars," in *War, Morality, and the Military Profession*, ed. Malham M. Wakin, 2nd ed. (Boulder, Colo: Westview Press, 1986), 227.

[9]Victor Davis Hanson, "Sherman's War," *American Heritage*, November 1999, 61. Emphasis in the original.

In using force to attain objectives, socially organized humankind must distinguish itself from other species. Thus:

> Shedding blood and killing are activities that no society can tolerate unless they are carefully circumscribed by rules defining what is, and is not, allowed. Always and everywhere, only that kind of killing which takes place by authorized persons, for specified ends, under approved circumstances, and in accordance with prescribed rules is saved from blame and is regarded as praiseworthy. Conversely, bloodshed which ignores the rules or violates them usually attracts punishment, atonement, or both.[10]

Yet retaliation, or "punishment," or "atonement" might well result even if the rules are followed scrupulously. Furthermore, the nature of the international system is such that actions taken frequently stimulate responses, in the same way as antibodies are produced in the human body to react to invasion by microorganisms.

Control means that the issues over which the use of force is contemplated or force is employed are political in nature and that the military means should be subordinated to political control. It is not without precedent that the use of military force has been uncontrolled, but certainly political leaders in democratic states will not willingly relinquish control to the military, for to forgo control is to relinquish power.

What constraints ought to be imposed on the use of force, and how they should be imposed has historically been a contentious subject. It was contentious in the large application of force over the former Yugoslavia in March–June 1999, and it was at issue in every use of force by Western, notably U.S., forces, in the twentieth century. The case is persuasive enough without looking in detail at the earlier record.

As a major participant in international interaction throughout the twentieth century, the United States has been conspicuous in its willingness to use force. Outside the two world wars that were fought in that century, the United States employed its military forces almost continuously—all over the globe. It conducted three major conflicts, all in Asia—in Korea, Vietnam, and Kuwait and Iraq. It undertook

---

[10]Martin Van Creveld, "The Persian Gulf Crisis of 1990–91 and the Future of Morally Constrained War," *Parameters* 22, 2 (Summer 1992): 38.

military operations in a variety of other places from Panama to Libya, Lebanon, and Afghanistan. This exceeds actions taken abroad by other states—even the colonial powers—by a wide margin.

Of interest, the United States has also found itself in the vanguard when the subject was fostering and embracing constraints on the use of force. Traditionally, restraint in statecraft was rooted in the interest of the contestants in being treated in the same way they opted to treat their adversaries. From time to time, new weapons were eschewed or condemned because of their inhumanity, and just before the turn of the twentieth century, states gathered at The Hague in the first formal international attempt to reach agreement on avoiding war.[11] Since that time, restrictions, not only on weapons but also on techniques for waging war, have been steadily gaining momentum.

As of 2002, there are 190 member states of the United Nations, an organization that boasted but fifty-one founding members in 1945. Being in large measure political experiments, some of those states will not endure. Some will, if history provides a minimal guide, be conquered by others. Some will collapse, falling into internal chaos and squalor. Some will merge with others. Many will change their form of government. Some will concede or surrender rather than fight,[12] but few to none will deliberately commit suicide. Unquestionably, on more than a couple, the jury is out on the question of their ultimate survival.

A sharp break exists between those who believe that the use of force is but one of the many instruments of statecraft in the international arena and those who contend that the use of force signifies a failure of policy. The former might be called *Clausewitzian;* the latter, *Anti-Clausewitzian.* It was Carl von Clausewitz who argued that war is "a continuation of political intercourse, carried on with other means."[13]

---

[11]Agreements among states to limit arms extend back at least as far as the Peloponnesian Wars in the fifth century B.C. Generally, they were included in bilateral peace treaties between states. The Hague marked the first convocation of states specifically for the purpose of "finding mutually acceptable means for avoiding war—rather than to liquidate a recent war." Blanche Weisen Cooke, Sandi E. Cooper, and Charles Chatfield, eds., *Arbitration or War? Contemporary Reactions to the Hague Peace Conference of 1899* (New York: Garland Publishing, Inc., 1972), 5.

[12]"It is easy to avert war if the government is willing to give the enemy what he wants." Richard K. Betts, *Surprise Attack: Lessons for Defense Planning* (Washington, D.C.: The Brookings Institution, 1982), 147.

[13]Carl von Clausewitz, *On War*, ed. and trans. Michael Howard and Peter Paret (Princeton, N.J.: Princeton University Press, 1976), 87.

Clausewitzians view war as fully integrated with, as a part of, policy; anti-Clausewitzians consider it a separate, aberrant phenomenon. Anti-Clausewitzians assess the use of force and violence on an international scale as they might evaluate the use of police power domestically—as a breakdown in law and order.[14] Clausewitzians, on the other hand, see the international use—or threat of use—of force as the natural concomitant of an international system devoid of a superior, overarching authority to maintain the peace.

If the use of force is considered to signal a breakdown in policy and to be an abnormal situation, then the desire seems natural to seek to limit severely its use and contain its effects. Even if it is thought of in Clausewitzian terms, however, force is the focal point of strong arguments that it should be used only with great care. The very existence of weapons of mass destruction (WMD), capable of causing great devastation of property and loss of life, calls out for stringent constraints on their use. Yet another serious paradox appears, for as Michael Howard points out, "Wars today can be irreversible in their consequences. There is thus little inclination to conduct them with restraint."[15] The circle with respect to deterrence is herewith closed: if wars can be irreversible, then deterrence has an even more difficult task.

The weight of evidence stands with those who identify a broad range of constraints and anticipate that they do, and will, have strong effect on the waging of combat operations. In the United States, recognition of the fact that civilized use of force requires that it be limited—in either Clausewitzian or anti-Clausewitzian terms—is clear. Constraints are real, and they have taken hold not only at the level of the policy making elites. According to the Army's field manual *Operations:*

> The people of the United States do not take the commitment of their armed forces lightly. They charge the government to commit forces only after due consideration of the range of options and likely outcomes. Moreover, the people expect the military to accomplish its

---

[14]They "speak as though mutual understanding, trust, and law should be able to replace the use of force in contemporary international affairs." James Finn, "Morality and Foreign Policy," in *Might and Right after the Cold War: Can Foreign Policy Be Moral?*, ed. Michael Cromartie (Washington, D.C.: Ethics and Public Policy Center, 1993), 42.

[15]Michael Howard, "Temperamenta Belli: Can War Be Controlled?" in *Restraints on War: Studies in the Limitation of Armed Conflict*, ed. Michael Howard (London: Oxford University Press, 1979), 6.

missions in compliance with national values. The American people expect decisive victory and abhor unnecessary casualties.[16]

What impact does the international security environment have on these issues? Has the international milieu become more benign or more chaotic? Are conditions more accommodating or more hostile to the use of force? The post-Cold War era has so far been remarkably unlike the postwar periods after World War I and World War II. One of the dissimilarities concerns the international mood. After those hot wars, the international desire was to banish war. Thus arose the Kellogg-Briand Pact, and immediately after the Second World War, the United Nations banned aggressive war, allowing the legitimate use of force only in self-defense.

Clearly, the Cold War, with its polarized antagonisms and concern for uncontrollable escalation, acted as a depressant on crisis and conflict.[17] Now, however, according to one expert:

> The prospect of major crises, even wars, in Europe is likely to increase dramatically now that the Cold War is receding into history. The next forty-five years in Europe are not likely to be so violent as the forty-five years before the Cold War, but they are likely to be substantially more violent than the past forty-five years.[18]

What is suggested for Europe must hold in spades for other, even more conflict-prone, areas of the world.

The possibility of conflict will not recede, but perhaps increase, in the future, and the use of force continues to be an option for sovereign states. Over time, however, the exercise of military power—in the West, and especially in the United States—has undergone two major changes. In the first place, expectations have changed. People in the West have altered the way they view the use of the military instrument. "Forty-odd

---

[16]Department of the Army, *Operations*, Field Manual 100-5 (FM 100-5) (June 1993), 1–2, 1–3.

[17]"To use force at all during the Cold War came to be seen almost everywhere as a very grave decision indeed, to be made only after the fullest deliberation, usually after all other means had been exhausted." Edward N. Luttwak, "Toward Post-Heroic Warfare," *Foreign Affairs*, May/June 1995, LEXIS-NEXIS, Dayton, Ohio: LEXIS-NEXIS (July 17, 1996).

[18]John J. Mearsheimer, "Why We Will Soon Miss the Cold War," in *Conflict after the Cold War: Arguments on Causes of War and Peace*, ed. Richard K. Betts (Boston, Mass.: Allyn and Bacon, 1994), 45.

years of ultra-stable nuclear peace have 'de-conditioned' Western society," according to Josef Joffe, "in the sense that expectations no longer include massive violence, either as a tool or a price of statecraft."[19] Others take this line of reasoning even further: "Among the 'modernist' states . . . new norms of behavior are replacing the old dictates of realpolitik: They reject not only the use of weapons of mass destruction, but even the use of military force to settle their disputes. . . . The modernist view clearly dominates in Western Europe, North America, parts of East Asia, and other regions."[20]

In the second place, the menu of constraints on the use of force has mushroomed. The sources and reasons for those constraints are many and diverse. For analytical purposes, they can be grouped into four categories: operational, organizational, legal, and moral. If, in fact, "[w]ars are won or lost," and "nations live or die primarily by the people's willingness to fight,"[21] then constraints on the willingness or ability to use force have a direct impact on the very survival interests of the state. These constraints have been increasing across the board, especially in the last decade.

These are not new developments.[22] Constraints have tended to grow with increasing U.S. international activity, however, keyed as they are to the U.S. interest in having its way in the world, but at the same

---

[19]Josef Joffe, "Democracy and Deterrence: What Have They Done to Each Other?" in *Ideas and Ideals: Essays on Politics in Honor of Stanley Hoffman*, ed. Linda B. Miller and Michael Joseph Smith (Boulder, Colo: Westview Press, 1993), 117.

[20]Barry Blechman and Cathleen S. Fisher, "Phase Out the Bomb," *Foreign Policy*, Winter 1994–1995, 81.

[21]Paul Seabury and Angelo Codevilla, *War: Ends and Means* (New York: Basic Books, Inc., 1989), 8.

[22]According to Geoffrey Best, "An inclination towards restraints and prohibitions in war is perceptible among enough of our species' earlier civilizations and/or cultures for the historian of humankind to regard it as essentially a normal aspiration, more or less as old as war itself." *War and Law since 1945* (Oxford: Clarendon Press, 1994), 15. Or, as Osgood and Tucker analyze the situation, "the change in men's attitude toward war, particularly as manifested by the need to justify force when it is resorted to, testifies to a growing sense of obligation that is potentially universal in scope. The wellspring of this sense of obligation is man's capacity for sympathy, and the force that gives this sense a potentially universal scope is man's capacity for reason, which enables him to comprehend mankind in its entirety and to act consistently with that comprehension. Despite the development of these faculties, men may of course still resort to force in their collective relations. In doing so, however, they find it increasingly difficult to remain indifferent to the effects of their behavior on others—even when the others are the adversary in war. The unease thereby experienced must somehow be appeased. At root, the need for justification is found in the desire to still this unease. It does not seem unreasonable to assume that the intensity of the need to justify force reflects the depth of this unease and, in consequence, must operate to impose progressive restraints on the measures men will be prepared to take against their fellows." Osgood and Tucker, *Force, Order, and Justice*, 197.

time to a concern about setting a positive example for others. States with less international ambition or less conscience suffer fewer inhibitions. Taken together, these are the taproots of asymmetrical warfare.

Asymmetries cause nightmares for strategists. Strategy is anticipation; successful strategists presage and then outwit their adversaries. Asymmetries arise if opponents enjoy greater freedom of action, or if they have weapons or techniques available to them that one does not. Perpetrators seek to avoid the strengths of their adversaries and to be unpredictable. They endeavor to take advantage of an ability to follow certain courses of action or to employ methods that can be neither anticipated nor countered effectively. Because asymmetries cause nightmares for strategists, they are most attractive to prospective adversaries.

"Asymmetrical warfare" is often used to describe a situation where an adversary can take advantage of its strengths or an opponent's weaknesses. The U.S. Joint Chiefs of Staff have defined asymmetrical warfare as "Attempts to circumvent or undermine an opponent's strengths while exploiting his weaknesses using methods that differ significantly from the opponent's usual mode of operations."[23]

But for the concept to be bounded reasonably, and to allow for conceptualizing about counters to it, asymmetrical warfare must be more finely tuned. Emphasizing one's strengths and exploiting an enemy's weaknesses is what strategy is all about. To view that as asymmetrical tends to trivialize a most vexing problem. True asymmetries, in contrast, are *those actions that an adversary can exercise that you either cannot or will not.*[24] These asymmetries are the breeding ground for those strategists' nightmares, for they comprise the most troublesome problems with which to deal.

---

[23]Franklin B. Miles, "Asymmetric Warfare: An Historical Perspective (Carlisle, Pa.: U.S. Army War College, 1999), 2–3. According to Kenneth F. McKenzie, Jr., "The first mention of the term was in the 1997 Quadrennial Defense Review (QDR) report." *The Revenge of the Melians: Asymmetric Threats and the Next QDR,* McNair Paper #62 (Washington, D.C.: National Defense University, 2000): 1. Metz and Johnson indicate an earlier, 1995, usage in Joint Publication 1, *Joint Warfare of the Armed Forces of the United States.* See Steven Metz and Douglas V. Johnson II, *Asymmetry and U.S. Military Strategy: Definition, Background and Strategic Concepts* (Carlisle Barracks, Pa.: Strategic Studies Institute, U.S. Army War College, January 2001), 2.

[24]McKenzie offers his own definition of asymmetrical warfare: "Leveraging inferior tactical or operational strength against American vulnerabilities to achieve disproportionate effect with the aim of undermining American will in order to achieve the asymmetric actor's strategic objectives." Ibid., 2. This definition, however, appears confined to the tactical and operational levels and specifies that the strength be inferior and employed against American vulnerabilities. In fact, asymmetrical warfare can involve a superior capability used strategically to negate an American strength, and it is not clear why these categories are excluded from McKenzie's definition.

True asymmetries pose grave difficulties for several reasons. First, because one cannot (or will not) respond in kind, offsetting tit-for-tat counteractions are impossible at worst, problematic at best. Second, asymmetrical attacks and defenses lean toward the countercultural. It is abhorrent to Western strategists even to contemplate some of the techniques or weapons of asymmetrical warfare. For these reasons, finally, the perpetrator of asymmetrical warfare will undoubtedly have surprise on its side. Cognitive dissonance of a horrific asymmetrical attack makes it difficult even to think through preparations for adequate defenses or counters. The intense struggle in the United States during the 1960s over civil defense against nuclear attack stands as a prime example in this regard, and the attacks against the World Trade Center and the Pentagon fall clearly into this pattern.[25]

What, specifically, constitutes asymmetrical warfare? Terrorism provides an excellent example. One must take care to understand what terrorism involves, however, and to use the term consistently. The definition ascribed to by the U.S. Federal Bureau of Investigation is: "the unlawful use of force and violence against persons or property to intimidate or coerce a government, the civilian population, or any segment thereof, in furtherance of political or social objectives."[26] This definition suffers from a glaring omission: namely, where's the terror? Nevertheless, the other essential elements are present: it is *unlawful, politically motivated,* and *directed against innocents* in order *to affect others.* As another important characteristic, "Terrorism . . . makes the decision to carry on acts of war and violence without accepting the limits of warfare."[27] This notion of actions *outside the limits imposed on the use of force* gives rise to the asymmetry.

The vicious, unprecedented attack on the United States on September 11, 2001, had not been entirely unforeseen or unanticipated.

---

[25]"Put simply, asymmetric threats or techniques are a version of not 'fighting fair,' which can include the use of surprise . . . and the use of weapons in ways unplanned by the United States. Not fighting fair also includes the prospect of an opponent designing a strategy that fundamentally alters the terrain on which a conflict is fought." National Defense University, Institute for National Strategic Studies, *Strategic Assessment 1998* (Washington, D.C.: National Defense University, 1998), 1. <http://www.ndu.edu/inss/sa98/sa98ch11.html> (Accessed October 2, 2000).

[26]28 C.F.R. Section 0.85. United States, Federal Bureau of Investigation, Counterterrorism Threat Assessment and Warning Unit, National Security Division, *Terrorism in the United States 1998*, i.

[27]Sidney Axinn, *A Moral Military* (Philadelphia: Temple University Press, 1989), 136.

The major shock lay in the means that were used: fully fueled airliners flown deliberately into buildings. This was an unambiguous demonstration of asymmetrical warfare, which defense analysts had envisioned for nearly a decade. The two important new aspects of asymmetric acts that so greatly increased their impact were the vulnerability of the U.S. homeland and the ability of individuals to gain control of instruments that could cause mass destruction.

The notion that the United States would not be attacked directly with military force became clear after the 1991 Gulf War. There the U.S. battlefield superiority was so great that Saddam Hussein fought asymmetrically—taking hostages, using human shields, destroying the environment with oil spills and fires, co-locating military targets with religious shrines and other targets proscribed by the Laws of Armed Conflict. This gave rise to speculation about "asymmetrical warfare" among military and defense analysts, which was broadly understood to encompass an adversary's taking advantage of his strengths and his enemy's weaknesses. The use of weapons of mass destruction—especially chemical and biological devices—and terrorism were generally included in the asymmetrical warfare warrior's arsenal. The reasoning was that enemies would be forced to use such nasty tactics because they would clearly lose a fair fight on a conventional military field of battle.

It was only dimly perceived that the ability to employ weapons of mass destruction (WMD)—traditionally understood to include chemical, biological, and nuclear—might be undertaken by nonstate individuals or groups. In the past, only organized states had access to such weapons, and they were carefully controlled. The devolution of control of such weapons to other than states represented a major change in the international security environment because the major barrier to their use had been deterrence. But against a terrorist group or bunch of religious fanatics, deterrence—either by threat of retaliation or by disallowing achievement of objectives—was an especially weak reed. If deterrence was ineffective against WMD use, then one must consider the other possibilities, of which there are but three: capitulation, preemption, or protection.

At about the same level of obscurity, a new concern was arising about the vulnerability of the U.S. homeland. If security means that citizens can exercise their freedoms without fear of attack—that is, if they enjoy a sanctuary from threats or attacks—then U.S. security was in increasing jeopardy. In part this was because of the increasing avail-ability of WMD to nonstate actors and the appearance of new forms of WMD—attacks on information, for example. In 1996–1997 a presi-dential commission conducted a broad study of the vulnerability of U.S. national infrastructure to attack from without or within. Their final report in October 1997 formally raised the alarm. But little had been done as of September 2001, and nothing, of course, to forestall what happened then.

In addition to terrorism, asymmetrical warfare comprises:

- hostage taking;

- biological, chemical, and radiological[28] warfare;

- deliberate wide-scale attacks on civilians;

- operational techniques, such as indiscriminate targeting; human wave or suicide attacks; emplacing anti-aircraft batteries on reli-gious shrines, schools, or hospitals; using human shields; booby traps—on wounded persons, for example; forms of information operations involving perfidy, false representation, or certain attacks against national infrastructure or computer networks; or, marching soldiers through minefields in order to clear the mines; and

- deliberate environmental destruction

because the United States and its Western allies cannot or will not practice them. All are beyond the limits on the use of force accepted by the United States and its closest friends and allies. So, while asym-metries are very difficult to reckon with, their source lies within limits and constraints willingly adopted. As a consequence, adversaries have at their disposal techniques and actions against which, in many cases, the United States stands paralyzed and powerless.

While the constraints, for the most part, have arisen from noble purposes, their cumulative effect on the ability of the United States to use force has provided both opportunity and impetus for asymmetrical

---

[28]Radiological weapons are those that cause harm through radiation alone, unaccompanied by the blast or heat of an atomic or nuclear yield. The materials can be delivered by a variety of nonnu-clear means, and they can be produced in any nuclear reactor, even small research reactors. There are no international controls on the manufacture, stockpiling, or use of radiological agents.

warfare. Any individual constraint can be defended, generally with logic and good sense. Separately, most are proper, reasonable, and worthwhile. But the whole in this instance is exceedingly greater than the sum of its parts. The cumulative weight of the constraints on the use of force, growing daily, has all but snuffed out U.S. freedom of action. It reduces flexibility, narrows options, diminishes available strategies, and tends to force more catastrophic choices rather than allowing more benign options. It requires the United States to operate on a field of action with increasingly greater unfavorable tilt.

It was suggested earlier that states do not knowingly commit suicide. Unwittingly, with very good intentions, the United States is moving along that path by amassing more and more constraints, depressing its willingness to fight, and stimulating asymmetrical acts by its adversaries.

Cumulatively, the constraints extinguish U.S. choices. By so doing, they accomplish the same effect as coercion by an enemy. Coercion is for the purpose of confining options, of requiring the target to do one's bidding. But their effect is unidirectional. "Surely," Seabury and Codevilla argue,

> No traditional Chinese or Indian manual of statecraft ever agonized over the legitimacy—as opposed to the prudence—of attacking a neighboring principality or of oppressing foreigners. Thus peace, the kind characterized by people treating each other more or less as they would like to be treated, is the peculiar and hard-won creature of Western minds. . . . This line of reasoning is shared by no other tradition.[29]

Or, as Michael Howard so trenchantly noted, "Agreed limitations on warfare imply rational understandings with an enemy who, if he can be reasoned with, should not be an enemy."[30] Thus, the myriad of constraints encourage adversaries to take asymmetrical advantage of the restraint they require, and in addition to tying the hands of U.S. military forces, provide a road map of U.S. vulnerabilities for adversaries and potential adversaries to follow.

---

[29]Seabury and Codevilla, War, 18.

[30]Howard, "Temperamenta Belli," in Howard, Restraints on War, 7.

The intention to take asymmetrical advantage of constraints on the use of force was nowhere clearer than in a book published in February 1999 in the People's Republic of China. Authored by two People's Liberation Army colonels, the text—entitled *Unrestricted Warfare*—offers specific advice to technologically disadvantaged forces that might come into conflict with the U.S. military. In an interview in June 1999, one of the authors asserted that "the first rule of unrestricted warfare is that there are no rules, with nothing forbidden."[31] He elaborated, arguing that strong countries would not use the same approach against weak countries because "strong countries make the rules while rising ones break them and exploit loopholes. . . . The United States breaks [U.N. rules] and makes new ones when these rules don't suit [its purposes], but it has to observe its own rules or the whole world will not trust it."[32]

Even though, at the present juncture, and for perhaps the next decade, the United States maintains military superiority over potential challengers, that does not mean that there are not provocateurs at large, waiting and watching. The one clear message they took from the 1991 Gulf War was not to engage the U.S. military directly. So, adversaries will look elsewhere for advantage—to embrace asymmetrical forms of warfare in order to capitalize on U.S. restraints.[33]

Clausewitz demonstrated sensitivity and insight with regard to this specific problem when he wrote

> The fact that slaughter is a horrifying spectacle must make us take war more seriously, but not provide an excuse for gradually blunting our swords in the name of humanity. Sooner or later someone will come along with a sharp sword and hack off our arms.[34]

---

[31]Quio Liang, quoted in the FBIS editor's note to the translation of Qiao Liang and Wang Xiangsui, *Unrestricted Warfare* (Beijing: PLA Literature and Arts Publishing House, 1999).

[32]Ibid.

[33]The naivete by which the United States applies the body of constraints is nowhere better described than in this anecdote: "General Hugh L. Scott, commanding the U.S. troops at Fort Bliss on the Mexican border, sent across the border to the insurgent leader, Pancho Villa . . . a pamphlet copy of 'The Hague Rules': the code of restraints on war by land which had been finally agreed on by the self-styled civilized nations in 1907. 'He spent hours poring over it. It interested and amused him hugely,' wrote John Reed. 'He said: "What is this Hague Conference? Was there a representative of Mexico there? . . . it seems to me a funny thing to make rules about war. It is not a game. What is the difference between civilized war and any other kind of war?" Geoffrey Best, "Restraints on War by Land before 1945," in Howard, *Restraints on War*, 17. Clearly, General Scott was sensitive to the tilt of the field of operations and sought to right it by sharing his rule book with the adversary.

[34]Clausewitz, *On War*, 260.

Importantly, one should ask: Are these constraints effective, or will they be discarded when the chips are down? According to one commentator, the military "would not be inclined to obey the rules that would cause them to lose a war."[35] A countersuggestion arose in the Gulf War when the Chairman of the U.S. Joint Chiefs of Staff asserted, "Decisions were impacted by legal considerations at every level."[36]

Worthy of note, some constraints adopted in peacetime have tended to evaporate when the smell of gunpowder was in the air. In some cases, this was done with great reservation and soul searching; at other times, they were shucked in a matter-of-fact fashion. When there was no direct strategic threat to the very existence of states, jettisoning constraints adopted in more pacific times was of no great import. The appearance of single weapons that can exterminate large segments of population, however, increases the ante on restraints. Asymmetrical threats involving WMD portend much graver consequences for unwarranted or unwise assumptions.

The questions linger, however: If constraints will be discarded when the issues are joined, what benefit is there to having them? Have WMD so increased the stakes that abiding by the imposed constraints might well produce apocalyptic results?

This study describes in detail the enormous variety of constraints over the use of military force by the United States, sets forth the effects of the growth of constraints, offers some remedies, and concludes on a hopeful note. For analytical purposes, the constraints have been organized into four categories: operational, organizational, legal—including arms control—and moral.

The strictures against any use of force, as well as efforts to modulate and constrain it, are complex and multidimensional. Many of the constraints imposed on the use of force originate in the deep and enduring belief that noncombatants, "innocents," should be immunized from the ravages of warfare. Clearly, this is not an idle concern, for, "Whereas in World War I, 5 per cent of the casualties were civilians, in World War II it was 50 per cent; in the latter part of the 1980s, 90 per cent of the casualties were civilians."[37] This theme runs strongly through all parts of

---

[35]Yves Sandoz, "Preface," in *The Technology of Killing: A Military and Political History of Antipersonnel Weapons*, Eric Prokosch (London: Zed Books, 1995), xiv.

[36]Steven Keeva, "Lawyers in the Room," *ABA Journal* 77 (December 1991): 52.

[37]Robert O. Muller, "Introduction," in Prokosch, *Technology of Killing*, ix.

the analysis, which emphasizes the external use of force by states of the international community. The arguments presented acknowledge, but neither scrutinize nor offer remedies for, the fact that wars are not the greatest killers of innocents. As R. J. Rummel points out, "While 36 million people have been killed in battle in all foreign and domestic wars in our century, at least 119 million more have been killed by government genocide, massacres, and other mass killing. And about 115 million of these were killed by totalitarian governments (as many as 95 million by communist ones)."[38] NATO's intervention in Kosovo in 1999 to curtail the "ethnic cleansing" of the Kosovar Muslims might mark a watershed in efforts taken to address this scourge. As a consequence of multidimensionality and deeply rooted themes, the chapters are significantly interrelated, and in some cases the decision to locate a particular constraint in one chapter instead of another was arbitrary.

In general, operational and organizational constraints on the use of force have been followed closely by legal and arms control regimes in order to discourage regression. Moral concerns, more than others, tend to be woven throughout, but in some cases, moral constraints have been imposed that bear scant relationship to operational, organizational, legal, or arms control considerations.

Let it be recorded that the central concern is neither to advocate avoidance of the use of force nor to remove all constraints on the use of force. The true prime objective is to seek ways to make the use of force unnecessary. But in order to do that, force must be usable, and it must be perceived by adversaries and prospective troublemakers as being usable. In this way the constraints cut to the heart of the issue: that force must be usable to be effective, and if it is perceived to be truly effective, then it will be less necessary. That is the inexorable chain of logic.

The first four chapters of the text that follows will address individually the wide variety of the sources of constraint. They have been grouped into four categories: operational, organizational, legal (including arms control), and moral. The intent is to reveal the broad scope and, in some cases, the fine detail of the constraints that have been imposed over the past hundred or so years. The constraints are presented in those four chapters in a straightforward way, the purpose being merely

---

[38]R. J. Rummel, "Political Systems, Violence, and War," *Command* 38, 1 (Spring 1989): 31.

to expose them. In Chapter 5, the effects of the myriad of constraints is analyzed. Here, the effort becomes more analytic, and more problematic. Chapter 6 then addresses remedies: What can and should be done to contain, and possibly to reverse, the process and rebalance the field of action? Here also, the suggestions are controversial, but the concluding chapter seeks to put them back into the perspective of what has happened since the end of the Cold War: the increasing layers and breadth of constraints have encouraged adversaries to adopt asymmetrical ways and means of attacking. It is not enough to recognize the inherent evil of such attacks and to respond to them. Because they have the potential for great—indeed unprecedented and horrible—harm, they must be prevented.

Well before the end of the Second World War, Winston Churchill observed,

> When peaceful people like the British and Americans, who are very careless in peacetime about their defense; carefree, unsuspecting nations and people who have never known defeat; improvident nations, I will say reckless nations, who despised military art and thought war so wicked that it never could happen again—when nations like this are set upon by highly organized and heavily armed conspirators who have been planning in secret over years on end, exalting war as the highest form of human effort, glorifying slaughter and aggression and prepared and trained to the last boundary which science and discipline permit, it is natural that the peaceful and improvident should suffer terribly, and the wicked, scheming aggressors should have their run of savage exultation.[39]

In the aftermath of the assaults on the United States of September 11, 2001, one marvels at the sagacity of these words, but one should also seek to ensure that the terrible suffering should never have to be experienced yet again.

---

[39]Winston Churchill, *New York Times*, October 12, 1942. Quoted in Irving M. Gibson, "Maginot and Liddell Hart: The Doctrine of Defense," in *Makers of Modern Strategy*, ed. Edward Mead Earle (Princeton, N.J.: Princeton University Press, 1943), 386.

CHAPTER 1

Operational Constraints

But once war is forced upon us, there is no other alternative than to apply every available means to bring it to a swift end. War's very objective is victory, not prolonged indecision. In war there is no substitute for victory.

General Douglas A. MacArthur

We have to ask the question, "Is the American public prepared for the sight of our most precious resources coming home in flag-draped caskets into Dover Air Force Base?"

General Henry Shelton, Chairman of the Joint Chiefs of Staff

Operational constraints on the use of force derive from "the American Way of War."[1] They have evolved over time, as experience, new technologies, and other considerations affect them. Operational constraints apply, in general, to what targets might be taken under attack, how, and when. This chapter describes operational constraints and their influence on thinking about current and prospective uses of military force.

The kinds of operational constraints under consideration here are the by-products of policy choices. Many other factors constrain the use of the military instrument: the weather, geography, and other environmental considerations; the physical performance characteristics of weapon systems; and the physiological and psychological bounds on human performance constitute the most important ones. These are not the kinds of constraints of interest to this analysis; rather, it is those that are undertaken as a matter of choice. It is recognized that the question of choice does not break out quite so easily. The physical performance capabilities of weapon systems is obviously also a matter of choice exercised in design, just as human performance can be the direct result of

---

[1]Russell F. Weigley, *The American Way of War: A History of United States Military Strategy and Policy* (New York: Macmillan, 1973).

choices made in training and preparation for combat. For the operator, however, those constraints are the result of prior decisions. Operational choices analyzed in this chapter takes those prior decisions as givens. "Prior decisions" appear later in this study as legal, arms control, or organizational constraints. Concerning U.S. military forces, the sources of operational constraint are fundamentally three in number: the strategic defensive; the relationship of military means to ways, ends, and risks; and reservations about the effects of the use of force.

Strategic Defensive

While it is common for adversaries of the United States to affix the label "imperialist" to its policies and international actions, the United States has no strategic designs on the territory of other states. It has no desire to dominate others politically and makes no plans to do so. In this century it has employed military force only in self-defense, not to attain objectives that would increase its territorial or economic assets. Its grand strategy, and that of the alliances and mutual defense pacts of which it is a part, operate on the strategic defensive. All major military operations in this century in which U.S. military forces participated were strategically defensive in nature: the First and Second World Wars, the Korean and Vietnam Wars, and the Coalition War Against Iraq (Operation Desert Storm). Even though NATO members were not directly attacked, moreover, the alliance acted defensively in 1999 in an attempt to protect the Kosovars from the depredations of the Serbian forces.

Looking at the 1974 United Nations General Assembly's definition of aggression:

> Any of the following acts, regardless of a declaration of war, shall be subject to and in accordance with the provisions of Article 2, qualify as an act of aggression:
>
> - The invasion or attack by the armed forces of a State of the territory of another State, or any military occupation, however temporary, resulting from such invasion or attack, or any annexation by the use of force of the territory of another State or part thereof;
>
> - Bombardment by the armed forces of a State against the territory of another State or the use of any weapons by a State against the territory of another State;

- The blockade of the ports or coasts of a State by the armed forces of another State;

- An attack by the armed forces of a State on the land, sea, or air forces or marine and air fleets of another State;

- The use of armed forces of one State which are within the territory of another State with the agreement of the receiving state, in contravention of the conditions provided for in the agreement or any extension of their presence in such territory beyond term of the agreement;

- The action of a State in allowing its territory, which it has placed at the disposal of another State, to be used by that other State for perpetrating an act of aggression against a third State;

- The sending by or on behalf of a State of armed bands, groups, irregulars or mercenaries, which carry out acts of armed force against another State of such gravity as to amount to the acts listed above, or its substantial involvement therein.[2]

The burden of proof would lie with those who would argue that the United States harbors designs to conduct aggression anywhere in the world. It should be noted, on the other hand, that many of these acts listed as "aggression" would be permitted if they were conducted in self-defense, in accordance with the U.N. Charter.

Strategically, the United States seeks only to defend its territory and interests, and those of its allies. Thus, the posture of the U.S. military is strategically defensive, and it is most unlikely to change. All U.S. military planning takes place in the context of strategic defensive operations. Many implications flow from this recognition, not the least of which is the inability to take advantage of strategic surprise, which in turn spawns difficulty in thinking about and anticipating strategic surprise.

In itself, the strategic defensive results in a serious constraint on the use of force. It means that the United States is willing, strategically, to absorb the first blow in a clash of arms. Notwithstanding the U.S.

---

[2]Cited in W. Michael Reisman and Chris Antoniou, eds., *The Laws of War: A Comprehensive Collection of Primary Documents on International Laws Governing Armed Conflict* (New York: Vintage Books, 1994), 10.

tactical doctrine of permitting its forces, through rules of engagement, to act defensively on detecting "hostile intent" on the part of an adversary, strategic first strike options are ruled out.[3] The result of this disposition has been the adoption of some militarily curious doctrines, which have led in some cases to operational constraints that must be considered no less than bizarre. In fact, the choices of constraints arose from genuine paradoxes, but the options were no less bizarre because of that.

Yet, the matter does not end with embracing a strategy of the defensive. Concurrently, pressures arise to ensure that one's adversaries are not threatened, because when they work the strategic calculus, they are obliged to consider hard capabilities, not intentions, which are much more elastic. So, in developing military capability to support the strategic defensive, one incurs certain obligations—through weapon design, deployments, operations, and exercises, as well as through doctrine—to convey defensive attitudes.[4]

This problem constantly plagued the North Atlantic Treaty Organization (NATO) in its desire to protect the center of Europe against a Warsaw Treaty Organization (WTO) attack. The European allies were concerned that the WTO not be threatened by NATO's forward-deployed forces, forces doctrinally not permitted to trade space for time. NATO doctrine demanded that the defense be staged well forward at the inter-German border; but it must look and act defensive, not offensive. Squaring this particular circle was made even more difficult by the imposition of overriding additional political constraints. For example, no powerful anti-tank defenses or barriers were permitted along the inter-German border because West Germany rejected physical impediments to its ultimate goal of reunification. Relocation of the forces stationed in the eastern part of West Germany to permit them to effect a stout defense from attacks from the East was also ruled out for political reasons. (The stationed forces were located essentially where they had stopped at the end of World War II; they were not optimally deployed to defend against a WTO attack.) Enhanced radiation weapons, neutron warheads

---

[3]The term "first strike" is invariably associated with a strategic nuclear attack. The term "first use" is often confused with it, but it means, literally, the first use of some capability—chemical weapons, for instance.

[4]This brings to mind the old saw about the British grenadier who, upon being asked what constitutes a defensive as opposed to an offensive weapon, responded: "I suppose it depends on which end you're standin'."

that promised to stop massed invasions of tanks dead in their tracks, were an emphatic political nonstarter in the Federal Republic of Germany. When it was pointed out that the defense could be made much stronger and deterrence bolstered by adding a counteroffensive capability, a firestorm of criticism greeted anyone who made such a suggestion.[5]

In summary, NATO was denied a broad range of operational options that might have been vital to a successful defense against a WTO attack. It could not erect stout territorial defenses, it could not relocate troops and bases to more advantageous territory, it could not adopt effective new technologies, and it could not counterattack. Essentially, any new scheme that would enhance NATO's chances of staving off a WTO attack was met with powerful political opposition.

With regard to long-range nuclear weapons, the difficulty of maintaining the strategic defensive arose from the potential for these kinds of weapons to execute a disarming first strike. Before the advent of intercontinental-range nuclear weapons, the notion of disarming an adversary in a single stroke was incomprehensible. Wars for high stakes were expected to be long and exhausting. But with the great power of the nuclear warhead, and with increasingly high probability of long-range single-shot kill, the possibility of a decisive strategic first strike became a reality. This marriage of nuclear weapons and long-range delivery capability was identified by Soviet authors in the 1960s as a "Revolution in Military Affairs."[6] The paradox arises from the fact that at the tactical and operational levels a disarming first strike is generally desirable: what better outcome can be projected than to disarm your adversary before he can strike you? At the strategic level, however, the acquisition of anything approaching a disarming first strike capability was resisted as very "destabilizing" and a prime engine of arms races.

The logic was that if one side possessed a disarming first strike, it would be tempted—especially in a crisis—to use it. Its adversary, therefore, was obliged to ensure that it did not offer the opportunity for a first strike, either by its mode of weapon deployment or by its actions. Its

---

[5]See, in particular, Samuel P. Huntington, "Conventional Deterrence and Conventional Retaliation in Europe," *International Security* 8, 3 (Winter 1983–1984): 32–56.

[6]A classic text on the subject is N. A. Lomov, ed., *Scientific Technical Progress and the Revolution in Military Affairs*, translated and published under the auspices of the U.S. Air Force (Washington, D.C.: U.S. Government Printing Office, 1974).

weapons must be made invulnerable–or, at least, highly survivable–so that a potential attacker would be deterred by the threat of a devastating retaliatory strike. Implicit, of course, was the signaled intention to absorb a first strike, thereby confirming the strategic defensive. Another obligation was to shun attempts to acquire a first-strike capability, thereby undermining one of the incentives for an arms race. Any relocation of forces or changes in alert states were criticized as threatening to crisis stability.

The instability of a disarming first strike capability, however, is operative only in the world of "Country A" and "Country B," which are artificial constructs for the strategic theorist. Within the value-neutral, metaphysical world of billiard-ball states identified only by letters and otherwise undifferentiated, the logic of arms races dominates. States and their leaders are held hostage, in this image, to the iron laws of the action-reaction cycle.[7] Yet, attempts to apply such abstractions to the real world leads to illogical and sometimes dangerous policies. Grant Hammond in his book *Plowshares into Swords*[8] strongly refutes the mechanistic interaction of arms resulting in "races" with historical research. And, in a classic study, Albert Wohlstetter[9] offered persuasive evidence that the mechanical, mindless, action-reaction cycle was never a part of U.S.–Soviet arms competition. But, for the United States at least, the logic prevailed in the case of intercontinental range nuclear weapons. Moreover, the specter of provoking "arms races" has been raised by those opposed to military forces incident to the proposed fielding of virtually every new weapon system or the expansion of existing ones. When the new administration of President George W. Bush suggested that a national ballistic missile defense should be fielded, for example, critics raised the alarm of new arms races because others would fear for their deterrents, which would stimulate additional proliferation.

---

[7]A typical assertion was made by Robert S. McNamara: "What is essential to understand here is that the Soviet Union and the United States mutually influence one another's strategic plans. Whatever their intentions or our intentions, actions—or even realistically potential actions—on either side relating to the buildup of nuclear forces necessarily trigger reactions on the other side. It is precisely this action-reaction phenomenon that fuels an arms race." Robert S. McNamara, *The Essence of Security: Reflections in Office* (New York: Harper and Row, 1968), 58.

[8]Grant T. Hammond, *Plowshares into Swords: Arms Races in International Politics, 1840–1991* (Columbia, S.C.: University of South Carolina Press, 1993).

[9]Albert J. Wohlstetter, *Legends of the Strategic Arms Race* (Washington, D.C.: U.S. Strategic Institute, 1975).

Adoption of "mutual assured destruction" (MAD) in the 1970s was the decided method of resolving the arms race paradox, in which the more arms a state amassed the more insecure it felt. According to this doctrine, U.S. weapons were, through a series of active and passive measures, to be made more resistant to first-strike attack. At the same time, hard-target counterforce weapons—those that can attack the weapons of the adversary—were to be eschewed in favor of small, penetrating weapons with capability only against soft, countervalue targets, specifically, centers of population and industry. Mutual assured destruction, a force-sizing measure that evolved mindlessly into strategy, required that sufficient secure long-range weapons be maintained so that a powerful retaliatory strike could be mounted even after absorbing an adversary's counterforce first strike.

Under mutual assured destruction, forces were sized in accordance with the MAD rubber ruler. In 1965 mutual assured destruction was said to require the capability to destroy one quarter to one third of the population plus two thirds of the industry of the Soviet Union after absorbing a Soviet first strike.[10] In 1967 the requirement changed to one fifth to one quarter population plus one half to two thirds industry.[11] Then in 1968 it was adjusted downward to one fifth to one quarter population plus one half industry.[12] The declining fractions reflected analysts' appreciation of the increases in the numbers, accuracy, and yield of Soviet weapons, reducing the residuals that would survive a first strike and thus be available for retaliation.

The prevailing mind-set of the time was that if a strategic force the size of a MAD force—defined by the current budget and adversary countermeasures—were retained, deterrence could not fail. To the question "What if deterrence were to fail?" the answer was "You don't understand. The purpose for building and retaining a mutual assured destruction force is to ensure that deterrence will not fail." To the follow-on question "OK, but what if deterrence nonetheless fails?" the answer invariably was the same: "The force is sized and constructed so

---

[10]United States, Department of Defense, *Report of the Secretary of Defense on the FY66–70 Defense Program* (Washington, D.C.: U.S. Government Printing Office, 1965), 39.

[11]United States, Department of Defense, *Report of the Secretary of Defense on the FY68–72 Defense Program* (Washington, D.C.: U.S. Government Printing Office, 1967), 39.

[12]United States, Department of Defense, *Report of the Secretary of Defense on the FY69–73 Defense Program* (Washington, D.C.: U.S. Government Printing Office, 1968), 50.

that deterrence *cannot* fail." The logic was circular and impenetrable. To some, it had the ring of deceit. "Instead of admitting that if minimum deterrence fails they prefer to surrender, they talk about all the damage that can be done to the Soviet Union by a few missiles. On what basis can this kind of dishonesty be justified? Are they not claiming a wisdom superior to that of the rest of the population and the right to pursue their ends by any means that succeed? Moreover, how can they fail to take into account the consequences if their deception is uncovered?"[13]

In fact, MAD had and has no answer for the failure of deterrence. It was a deterrent strategy, pure and simple, one that sought deterrence in the threat to annihilate millions of civilians and devastate an adversary's industrial infrastructure. It was the creature of the kind of operations analysis that stems from apolitical "Country A" and "Country B" approaches and the offspring of purely rational analysis that seeks to determine, quantitatively, how much is enough. For the most part, the military favored counterforce capability—the Air Force for its clear military value and desirability in damage limitation,[14] and the Navy (early in the nuclear weapons debate) because of its aversion to countervalue city-busting weapons.[15] But Pentagon civilians, fortified by arms controllers, prevailed in imposing this operational constraint at the strategic level.

A by-product of the MAD logic sequence was the abandonment of strategic defenses, both passive (civil defense) and active (strategic air

---

[13]Morton A. Kaplan, *Strategic Thinking and Its Moral Implications* (Chicago: The University of Chicago Center for Policy Study, 1973), 9.

[14]The term "damage limitation" refers to destroying the weapons of the enemy in order to limit the damage they can wreak on oneself. It is a subset of counterforce.

[15]For example, this testimony of Rear Admiral Ralph Ofstie: "It is time that strategic bombing be examined relative to our own American principles, to the decent opinions of mankind, and to the traditions of civilization. . . . There has been a great deal of talk about 'survival in the air age.' Survival of what? If we mean the bare and simple physical survival of American lives, the answer is easy. Do not fight at all. But if we mean the survival of the values, the principles, and the traditions of human civilization, we must insure that our military techniques do not strip us of our self-respect. If we consciously adopt a ruthless and barbaric policy towards other peoples, how can we prevent the breakdown of ethics and morality in our domestic affairs? The concept of indiscriminate atomic attacks on non-military targets undermines our accepted values and if it is initiated may destroy them." "Views on Question 7 of the Agenda of the House of Representatives Committee on Armed Services Investigation on Matters Pertaining to the B-36 bomber," August 20, 1949, B-9, *Agenda Manual*, Section III, Op-23 Files, 21.

and ballistic missile defenses). Thomas Schelling, for example, wrote: "I like the notion that East and West have exchanged hostages on a massive scale and that *as long as they are unprotected*, civilization depends on the avoidance of military aggression that could escalate to nuclear war."[16] Once the logic of MAD had been accepted and it was believed that defenses against intercontinental nuclear weapon-carrying vehicles would not be effective, and given the fiscal attractiveness of MAD, strategic defenses were believed to be irrelevant, destabilizing, or both. First the continental air defense system was almost completely dismantled, then civil defense was all but abandoned, and, finally, effective strategic ballistic missile defenses were surrendered at the SALT I negotiating table.

The ABM Treaty of 1972 enshrined mutual assured destruction by preventing the sides from deploying more than very light strategic defenses against missile attack. This highlighted another noteworthy paradox: the state with a clear and avowed defensive strategy willingly bargained away the instrument that would safeguard that strategy: strategic defense.

Supported by a morbid strain of logic—"The threat of retaliation deterred Joseph Stalin and Mao. Everybody recognizes that if you launch a nuclear attack on the United States, we would turn that country into a sea of radioactive glass in 30 minutes"[17]—MAD succeeded in causing strategic defenses to be renounced. Yet, turning another state into "a sea of radioactive glass" could not redress the damage that would be done. It had no satisfactory answer for the open questions: "What does one do if deterrence fails?" "What can be done if the Department of Defense does not fulfill its fundamental objective to defend the American people?" and "How can retaliation compensate in any way for the tremendous loss of life suffered by absorbing a nuclear attack?"

Beyond the inability to field strategic defenses, by embracing a strategic defensive doctrine, the United States imposes other constraints on the acquisition of certain weapons and the evolution of doctrine for their use. For example, little emphasis has been accorded to

---

[16]Thomas Schelling, "What Went Wrong with Arms Control?" *Foreign Affairs*, Winter 1985–1986 233. Emphasis added.

[17]John Pike, Union of Concerned Scientists, quoted in Rowan Scarborough, "Missile Attack on U.S. Called Very Unlikely," *Washington Times*, December 12, 1991, A10.

offensive heavy tank warfare, and—until late in the Cold War—deep offensive strikes. This might not be lamented, given the absence of territorial designs on other states. But the confusion projected downward from the strategic level to other levels of warfare does give rise to a variety of problems. Powerful offensive weapons have great utility at the operational and tactical levels. They are needed to support reactive operations as part of strategic defensive campaigns.

Preemptive attack—to forestall an impending attack by an adversary—is neither illegal nor immoral, but difficult even to contemplate under the mantle of the strategic defensive.[18] *Preventive* attack—to forestall an adversary's gaining a particular capability, or even to prepare for an attack—has fallen far below any interest in preemptive attack. As a matter of curiosity, the Israeli preventive attack on the Iraqi *Osirak* nuclear reactor in 1981 was roundly denounced—even the Reagan administration voted against its attack in the United Nations. Yet, in the Gulf War, the United States and its coalition allies benefited directly from the Israeli operation a decade earlier. An open question asks: What are the odds that such an effort as Desert Storm would even have been attempted if Saddam Hussein had had an arsenal of nuclear weapons?

Although much hue and cry is heard about the potential for "rogue states" or terrorists to acquire weapons of mass destruction, the measures contemplated against them have been, in the main, administrative, not operational. "It is far from accidental," writes Patrick Glynn, "that, since the Gulf war, the major calls for violent U.S. intervention against renegade states—calls of major air attacks against Serbia and Serb forces in Bosnia, for arms shipments to the Bosnian Muslims, and for preemptive strikes against North Korean nuclear facilities—have gone unheeded."[19] It took the shock of the September 11, 2001, attacks with a new form of weapon of mass destruction, a civilian airliner fully loaded with fuel, to prompt the government to undertake preventive operations against future terrorist attacks, starting in Afghanistan. It should be clear that the operations against the terrorists were less retaliatory in nature than a form of preventive self-defense.

---

[18]Interestingly, the 1992 U.S. *National Military Strategy* argued that the United States must be able to apply force preemptively, "in order to defuse a crisis," but the 1995 and 1997 versions were mute on the subject. United States, Joint Chiefs of Staff, *National Military Strategy of the United States,* (Washington, D.C.: U.S. Government Printing Office, January 1992), 16.

[19]Patrick Glynn, "Quantum Leap," *The National Interest* (Spring 1995): 55.

So, a strategic defensive posture depresses interest and preparation for preemptive or preventive attack. By so doing, it also increases the possibility of being surprised. This forms a major concern for the future because surprise maintains pride of place as a key principle of warfare. It can have decisive effects at all levels and stands as a "force multiplier" par excellence. Inferior forces know that they can gain an advantage when confronting a superior adversary by the use of surprise. Thus, it is very attractive to them. But surprise is not a proprietary asset of the inferior. It works for superior forces as well. The strategic defensive, looking to preserve military capability and defend targets rather than actively to attack potential aggressors, makes adversarial surprise more likely and its effects more telling. It also depresses interest in, and activity focused on, taking the strategic initiative.

As noted by Edward Luttwak, "To use force at all during the Cold War came to be seen almost everywhere as a very grave decision indeed, to be made only after the fullest deliberation, usually after all other means had been exhausted."[20] Thus it can be seen that this issue extends beyond the question of the strategic defensive, which says that one will not be the first to use force, to the question of the *ultima ratio*, that the use of force can be contemplated only "after all other means," or as a last resort. The question of the use of force as a last resort will be entertained in Chapter 3.

Relationship of Means to Ways, Ends, and Risks

The *means* of warfare, or the instruments, bear a close relationship to the *ways* they are used to attain the *ends*, or the goals of warfare. Often, the means dictate the ways. For example, if a state has no navy—and no practical method of acquiring one—then maritime blockade is not an available option. Means dictating ways is the source of the aphorism that "If all you have is a hammer, all problems tend to look like nails." In an ideal world, once the use of force has been decided upon, national authorities prescribe the political and military ends to be sought. Military leaders then take the means they have been provided and develop ways to attain those ends. In a dialogue between political and military leaders, a way (or strategy) is selected, one that appears capable of attaining the ends at an acceptable level of risk. Risk arbitrates between

---

[20]Luttwak, "Toward Post-Heroic Warfare," 110.

ways, ends, and means. Some ways are riskier than others to attain the same ends with the same means. Likewise, the employment of some means are riskier than others to attain the same ends in the same way. In the real world, however, things do not always work this way.

Operational constraints burgeon when ends are limited, for so then must ways, means, and risks be carefully limited. Conversely, and importantly, "Once men abandon themselves to unrestrained violence the interests they thereby jeopardize must also become unlimited."[21] For the United States, the conceivable ends of warfare—or its objectives—will inevitably be limited. There is irony here, for at a time when weapons have made it possible for the United States to pursue unlimited ends against all but one state in the world—Russia—the prospects of using such a capability approach zero. Indeed, the days of unconditional surrender are long past, for there are no conceivable objectives that would appear to require such extreme measures. Such a statement is too unqualified for many other states in the world (Israel, South Korea, and Taiwan come to mind), but remains valid for the United States. This gives rise to an important operational asymmetry in which one side might be concerned about survival interests, while the other would be operating on the basis of interests much lower on the scale.[22] The higher up the scale of interests one believes himself to be, the less likely his objectives will be constrained. Put slightly differently, the lower the level of perceived interests, the more actions will tend to be adjudged as discretionary. Objectives related to national survival will not be viewed as discretionary, while initiatives for purely humanitarian reasons will be considered wholly as a matter of discretion.

It was not so very long ago that it was asserted that merely maintaining the ability to employ unlimited means meant that no ends ever needed to be forsaken. The words of Philip Green, barely twenty-odd years old, sound anachronistic today: "The availability of nuclear weapons for use, and the acceptance of that availability by the theorist, insures that no military problem need ever be thought of as being totally without a military solution, and no goal need ever be totally surrendered."[23] In fact,

---

[21]Osgood and Tucker, *Force, Order, and Justice*, 199.

[22]Donald Nuechterlein usefully analyzes state interests in four categories: survival, vital, major, and peripheral in *America Overcommitted* (Lexington, Ky.: University of Kentucky Press, 1985).

[23]Philip Green, "Strategy, Politics, and Social Scientists," in Kaplan, *Strategic Thinking*, 45.

however, the range of goals, the accomplishment of which is safeguarded by nuclear weapons, tends to be narrow for the United States, not wide. It is difficult to conceive of the employment of nuclear weapons, for example, except in the most dire circumstances in which U.S. survival, or the survival of a treaty ally, was at stake. The image is strong: there can be no victors in a nuclear war, and this is an accepted truth even if only one side has nuclear weapon capability.

The relationship between ends and means has been grossly distorted by the embrace of mutual assured destruction—discussed earlier in this chapter—in the strategic nuclear relationship between the superpowers during the Cold War. As Michael Howard pointed out,

> Western strategists plan for the mass destruction of Soviet cities, and vice versa, not because their political masters have any serious political motive for extirpating the societies of their adversaries, but because in a grotesque inversion of logic the means now dictate the ends.[24]

Those who adopted mutual assured destruction as the central strategic tenet of the U.S.–Soviet strategic relationship were not thinking strategically, however. They had political and budgetary fish to fry.

Just as threatening with unlimited means was intended to be so frightening that peace, and stability, would thereby be ensured, constraining means can convey to potential adversaries the limits of one's intentions. More than weapon acquisition is involved, however. Clearly, if a state has no long-range bombers and no other long-range attack capability, its means limit the ends it can accomplish. Beyond orders of battle—or inventories of weapons—system maintenance, training exercises, and operational deployment provide messages about one's overall military capability and intentions. Decisions are made by military planners, based on their observations of adversary military activity and preparation. If a potential adversary has never been observed to exercise its air defenses, then one would be justified in believing that those air defenses will probably operate ineffectively when put to the test. Operational limitations on one's own forces, therefore, can arise from not acquiring certain capability, and also by not maintaining, exercising, and deploying it.

---

[24]Howard, "Temperamenta Belli," in Howard, *Restraints on War*, 8.

Ends, means, ways, and risks are also relational. That is, they must be related to a particular adversary or task. Means that would suffice against one adversary might fail totally against another. Risks that might be run against one foe might be unacceptable against another. As adversaries become stronger, or as one's own capability becomes relatively weaker, one becomes more reluctant to use force because the risks will have increased. One might not be willing to risk a very expensive weapon against a second-rate adversary because to lose the expensive weapon would seem wasteful, would deplete the arsenal against more severe threats, and would devalue the weapon in the eyes of a first-rate enemy.[25]

The reasons for limitations tend to be strongly situation-dependent, as they should be, but over time, efforts have been devoted to providing guidelines. One hotly debated example of an attempt to provide such guidelines was the so-called Weinberger Doctrine:

- The United States should not commit forces to combat unless our vital interests are at stake. Our interests, of course, include interests of our allies.

- If the United States decides that it is necessary to commit its troops to combat in a specific situation, we must commit them in sufficient numbers and with sufficient support to win. If we are unwilling to commit the forces or resources necessary to achieve our objectives, or if the objective is not important enough, we should not commit our forces.

- If we do decide to commit forces to combat, we must have clearly defined political and military objectives. Unless we know precisely what we intend to achieve by fighting, and how our forces can accomplish those clearly defined objectives, we cannot formulate or size forces properly, and we should not commit our forces at all.

- The relationship between our objectives and the forces we have committed—their size, composition, and disposition—must be continually reassessed and adjusted as necessary.

---

[25]"The B-2 is too sophisticated for war," wrote columnist William Pfaff. "Its very cost blocks its use." "The Pentagon's Ultimate Weapon Too Wonderful to Use," *Baltimore Sun*, October 9, 1995, 21.

- Before the United States commits combat forces abroad, the U.S. government should have some reasonable assurance of the support of the American people and their elected representatives in the Congress.

- Finally, the commitment of U.S. forces to combat should be a last resort—only after diplomatic, political, economic and other efforts have been made to protect our vital interests.[26]

These criteria were not universally accepted, even within the U.S. government—then-Secretary of State George Shultz took strong public exception to them—and they need not detain this analysis. Suffice it to say at this juncture that limited ends dictate limited ways and means to achieve them. The operational limitations might be related to the available means—no AWACS aircraft was available for employment, or no anti-tank weapons could be brought to the scene quickly enough, for example. The operational limitations might also be the result of choices of ways—the target would be attacked on east-west axes to avoid flying over neutral territory, or, as was the case in Vietnam, for example, to avoid flying over the potentially hostile People's Republic of China. Indeed, of all the bombs dropped in Indochina by U.S. forces, the lion's share was *not* dropped on North Vietnam.[27]

It should be clear that some ends involve such high risks that no ways or means would be able to achieve them. The point is that the rational use of force by the United States in the future contains its own self-limitations and constraints. The fact that the United States has only scant threats to its survival, and only low-grade threats to its vital interests, helps to ensure that the use of force will be heavily constrained from its very inception.

---

[26]These were first set forth in a speech to the National Press Club, delivered on November 28, 1984, and reported in the *Washington Post*, November 29, 1984, p. A1, passim. This list is extracted from Caspar Weinberger, *Annual Report of the Secretary of Defense, Fiscal Year 1987* (Washington, D.C.: U.S. Government Printing Office, 1988), 78–79.

[27]"Some 6,162,000 tons of bombs were dropped by Air Force fighter-bombers and bombers in Southeast Asia—almost triple the 2,150,000 tons dropped during World War II and far exceeding the 454,000 tons dropped during the Korean War, but these figures are misleading. Many were wasted bombing holes in the jungle in an ineffective interdiction campaign, and less than 1,000,000 tons were dropped on North Vietnam itself." Harry G. Summers, *On Strategy II: A Critical Analysis of the Gulf War* (New York: Dell, 1992), 107–108.

The same may not be true of adversaries of the United States. As noted above, they might be engaged for higher stakes—or they might believe that they are engaged for higher stakes—than the United States. Unlike the United States, they might consider the contest to be one of survival; they might not have subscribed to the same rule book. In fact, if they consider themselves militarily inferior, they will look for asymmetrical solutions to their security problems, avoiding the need to go head-to-head with superior U.S. or coalition forces.[28] Likewise, adversaries might be willing to conduct war in ways the United States is not, and they might well have very different propensities for risk taking. This subject will be revisited in Chapter 5.

Finally, estimates throughout the process of developing ends, ways, means, and assessing risks are notoriously difficult to make. Even though weapons undergo rigorous testing, many of them—even entire classes of armament—have never been employed in anger. So, like the U.S. torpedo failures at the beginning of World War II, one must hold reservations about whether hardware will perform as advertised, or even as tested and exercised. Moreover, as systems become more and more complex, and as adversaries approach the level of peer competitors, the difficulty of the estimation process increases. Assessment of the effects of information operations,[29] for example, is particularly troublesome.

When ends, ways, and means are poorly coordinated, high risks ensue. Objectives that exceed the capability of the forces available to accomplish them, or strategies that ask for too much of forces assigned do not inspire high confidence in possibilities for success. Such discontinuities or mismatches between ends, ways, and means will continue to plague U.S. decision makers. A large measure of the art of war is to find creative ways to bring ends, ways, and means into harmony. While

---

[28]This inspired Martin Van Creveld to write, "The attraction of gas stems from the ease with which it is manufactured and, paradoxically, the special horror in which it is held. Further, since it does not destroy property, it is well suited for governments to punish their own rebellious subjects without causing widespread internal damage. In the face of these considerations, the rule which prohibits its use—particularly in conflicts inside and between third world countries—is likely to prove fragile." "Persian Gulf Crisis," 28.

[29]Information operations comprises electronic warfare, military deception, psychological operations, operations security, computer network attack and defense, and physical destruction of an adversary's information infrastructure. Combat assessment of the effects of attacking such capabilities are particularly difficult, especially because they are often not directly observable, and, consequently, the adversary will take every effort to thwart assessment.

adversaries will no doubt labor under similar problems, they might have greater tolerance for mismatches, and hence for risk. Solutions to balancing ends, ways, and means that are available to adversaries, but not to one's own approach to conflict, lie in asymmetrical forms of warfare.

Reservations about the Effects of the Use of Force

Deep reservations about effects hinder even the contemplation of the use of force. In the first place, assessments of the effectiveness of the use of force have always been daunting. It inevitably involves costs and risks that, along with payoffs or benefits, are very difficult to calculate. Moreover, pessimism seems to dominate once one begins to look carefully at potential uses of the military instrument. Thus, for example, "targeting enemy leaders often proves infeasible, people immoral, and resources wasteful."[30]

The use of force can be measured in three dimensions: intensity, geographic scope, and time. Those who plan for the use of force find that they must think about how to economize in each dimension. They must consider how to keep any employment of military force to the minimum intensity required to succeed without unacceptable risks. Considerations about the intensity of effects, for example, have removed the use of any weapon of mass destruction (nuclear—except in retaliation—chemical, radiological, or biological) from consideration in U.S. operations. But it has reached even farther down, to the banning of, for example,

- hollow-nosed (dum-dum) bullets,
- bullets designed to flatten, tumble while on their trajectory, or fragment after hitting their target,
- projectiles filled with glass, and
- napalm.

Now, increased pressure is being put on weapons such as cluster bombs and depleted uranium projectiles—the former because they are indiscriminate, and the latter because they purportedly pollute the environment and are carcinogenic if ingested by humans. Intensity is controlled as well by the other factors: organizational, legal, and moral.

---

[30]John Arquilla, "Strategic Implications of Information Dominance," *Strategic Review* (Summer 1994): 28.

Planners must analyze how to confine the use of force geographically in order neither to destroy more than is necessary nor to spread conflict without sufficient justification. This includes great and increasing concern for not damaging the ecology or other aspects of the environment. "Spreading the conflict," while strategically sound as a way to take the fight to a location where the enemy did not want to fight and thereby to negate some of his advantages, the concept of "horizontal escalation" was roundly criticized when it was put forth in the first Reagan administration.[31] Mines, both land and sea versions, are devices that alter the usable geography. Arms control and legal strictures have significantly reduced the operational utility of mines, however.[32]

Finally, planners must find ways to accomplish the objectives of the use of force in minimum time; U.S. low tolerance for high levels of carnage means prolongation of hostilities—a strategy used with decisive effect by North Vietnam—will rarely be desirable. In times past, economic considerations held sway when it came to capping the length of war. Osgood and Tucker remark that "Throughout the eighteenth century, war on land and at sea had to be attenuated or terminated because it threatened financial ruin, owing to the destruction of commerce at sea and to the expense of keeping armies and navies fighting."[33] In contrast, strategic nuclear war would be short and devastating.[34]

For some, the use of force is almost never justified. Anti-Clausewitzians view it as a failure of policy, rather than as a continuation of policy. They argue that force will not resolve problems; or if it will, it will be too costly. Other options will invariably be preferable, they contend. And they provide constant reminders of the possibility of retaliation, the shortcomings of intelligence, the negative reactions of onlook-

---

[31]See Joshua Epstein, "Horizontal Escalation: Sour Notes of a Recurrent Theme," *International Security* 8 (Winter 1983–1984): 19–31.

[32]A global effort to ban antipersonnel land mines has focused attention on the use of such mines by U.S. forces. Reacting to these pressures, President Clinton announced in 1996 that U.S. forces may no longer employ non-self-destructing antipersonnel land mines except for training and on the Korean Peninsula—to defend against an armed attack across the Demilitarized Zone. In addition, Protocol II of the 1980 Conventional Weapons Convention, to which the United States is a party, contains restrictions on land mines.

[33]Osgood and Tucker, *Force, Order, and Justice*, 46.

[34]It was parodied by the work of Tom Lehrer, among others: "So long, Mom, I'm off to drop the bomb, so don't wait up for me. . . . Look for me when the war is over, an hour and a half from now!" *Too Many Songs by Tom Lehrer* (New York: Pantheon Books, 1981), 116–118.

ers (friends, adversaries, others), the pain of casualties, and the difficulty of terminating hostilities once begun. Any contemplated use of force will evoke these counterarguments.[35]

Despite such counterpressures, U.S. decision makers have found justification for the defensive use of force, especially if it is suitably limited and controlled. Appropriate limitations and controls involve concern about finding and attacking the right targets, minimizing collateral damage and unintended effects, and suffering casualties.

Much effort and analysis attends target selection. After all, if an adversary's corporate heart, or brain, or central nervous system can be attacked directly, why attack a limb? In the past, it was generally sufficient to attack military forces that were in close proximity to one's own; for neither weapon systems, nor surveillance systems, nor intelligence networks would support targeting far beyond the immediate battlefield. Today, however, the advent of global surveillance and precision long-range striking systems allow those who possess them to attack nearly any target at any time. One does not have to be limited to targets that expose themselves or that are convenient. The difficulty arises when key targets cannot confidently be identified, or if identified, cannot be located, or if identified and located, cannot be attacked for other reasons.

In fact, the high accuracy with which U.S. forces can attack provides a constraint on their use. As recently as the Second World War, targeters were happy if they could hit a target the size of a small city. More recently, say in Vietnam, striking within a couple of city blocks of a target was considered the norm. Today, it's a question of which window in a building the weapon should fly through. Whereas in 1943 it took 1,500 B-17 sorties dropping six one-ton bombs each to destroy a 60-by-100-foot target with 90 percent probability of kill (Pk), by 1970 in Vietnam the same size target required 176 F-4 Phantom sorties to achieve the same Pk. Today, one laser-guided bomb delivered by one

---

[35]Samuel Huntington put it presciently: "The argument has been made, for instance, that whatever the merits of retaliating or not retaliating in response to terrorist attacks, the U.S. should not retaliate because inevitably that action will be goofed up, the wrong targets will be hit, civilian casualties will be excessive, American losses will be too great, and the whole effort will end in humiliation and be counterproductive to boot." "Playing to Win," *The National Interest* (Spring 1986): 12. All of these contentions were raised post-September 11, 2001, when actions against terrorism were being considered.

F-117 (10 foot circular error probable [CEP]) is all that is required. Yet, such precision brings its own constraints because it elevates concern about acceptable results,[36] collateral damage, and unintended consequences. Questions are raised about the specific importance and value of targets that could never even have been contemplated at a time when such targets could not be discriminated, much less selectively hit. In this way, precision brings its own set of constraints.

Those who are philosophically opposed to the use of force, however, have not welcomed the appearance of very accurate weapons. Just to demonstrate that the logic can be twisted almost without limit:

> In the West . . . there is an influential body of opinion that holds that the more discriminating and less collaterally damaging a weapon is, the more immoral it must necessarily be. This is because its very effectiveness and reasonableness make it more likely to be used.[37]

This paradox has plagued weapon acquisition in the United States since the founding of the Union. Its roots lie deep within the aversion to any use of force. On the one hand, the argument emphasizes pursuit of accurate weapons because they have fewer undesirable effects. On the other hand, if one acquires highly accurate weapons with good prospects of successfully attacking a target while avoiding collateral damage and unintentional consequences, the threshold for using force might well be lowered. Decision makers, thus, would be tempted by the prospects of lower risks and costs to use force—perhaps even when they should not.[38] A genuine paradox, it appears fundamentally irresolvable.

---

[36]"In its Desert Storm white paper, the Air Force reported that campaign planners' faith in the F-117 targeting system was so great that pilots were tasked to hit not merely a particular building or shelter 'but a particular corner, a vent, or a door.' In fact, if they hit the building, but not the particular spot, their sortie counted as a miss, not a hit." U.S. General Accounting Office, *Operation Desert Storm: Evaluation of the Air Campaign*, NSIAD-97-134 (Washington, D.C.: General Accounting Office, 1997), 5.2.2.

[37]Seabury and Codevilla, *War*, 238.

[38]"Seemingly tailor-made for an era of post-modern politics, precision weapons also have the potential to increase the propensity of political leaders to resort to violent means. The ready availability of [PGMs] may tempt them to conclude that force need no longer remain the option of last resort, and induce them to employ their arsenal without due reflection." A. J. Bacevich and Lawrence F. Kaplan, "The Clinton Doctrine," *The Weekly Standard*, September 30, 1996, 20–21, quoted in Charles J. Dunlap, *Technology and the Twenty-First-Century Battlefield: Recomplicating Moral Life for the Statesman and the Soldier* (Carlisle, Pa.: U.S. Army War College, January 15, 1999), 26.

Target selection is a two-way street. Adversaries will be conducting their own targeting as well and will be aware of one's targeting effort. This means that they will seek to prevent targeting of their key or vital nodes, while attempting to identify and target those of their attacker. They will also seek to take asymmetrical advantage of their enemy's perceived targeting proclivities and restraints.

Adversaries might be essentially insensitive to collateral damage—whether inflicted on them or that which they cause. They might, as Saddam Hussein did, collocate military targets with those that are on the prohibited list: religious shrines, schools, hospitals, or places of cultural or artistic value, for example. They might also, as Saddam Hussein did, take hostages or prisoners of war and use them as human shields, or cause excessive damage to the natural environment—asymmetrical actions, all.

It is not only collateral damage from attack that acts as an inhibitor. Concern for "unintended consequences" has also become a factor. An unintended consequence might involve the inadvertent pollution of an adversary's water supply or destruction of records of immunization, to cite two random examples. Unintended damage to the environment has become a concern, not just in using force, but also in training and exercising military units. Clearly, also, blue-on-blue engagements (mistakenly attacking friendly forces) qualifies as an unintended consequence.

Among the strongest of U.S. constraints is sensitivity to taking and imposing casualties. According to Edward Luttwak, "the risk of suffering casualties is routinely the decisive constraint."[39] Elsewhere, Luttwak links high prospective casualties directly to decisions on the kind and number of forces to position in a crisis: "The prospect of high casualties, which can rapidly undermine domestic support for any military operation, is the key political constraint when decisions must be made on which forces to deploy in a crisis, and at what levels."[40] If Luttwak is correct that anticipated casualties are foremost in decision makers' minds, and if they have anything like Weinberger's criteria informing their decisions when they contemplate the use of force in a crisis, then the range of options available to deal with crises appears very narrow indeed.

Still, estimates of casualties are not easy to make. The difficulty in estimating potential casualties in conflict was never more powerfully on

---

[39]Luttwak, "Toward Post-Heroic Warfare."

[40]Edward N. Luttwak, "A Post-Heroic Military Policy," *Foreign Affairs*, July–August 1996, 36.

display than in the ramp up to Operation Desert Storm. Casualty estimates ranged from a few hundred up to fifteen thousand,[41] but the actual casualty levels were only a small fraction of most estimates.[42] Nevertheless, the constraint is pertinent. It has operational effects, as in the conduct of air operations over Kosovo and Serbia in 1999 when aircraft were restricted to a floor of 15,000 feet so that minimum casualties would result.[43] In the extreme, casualty avoidance might become the key determinant of whether or not to use force.

As noted previously, evidence is growing that more and more civilians, or noncombatants, have been bearing a greater and greater burden when it comes to casualties in war. This illustrates, inter alia, the trend away from conflicts being fought exclusively by formal armies located on designated battlefields, waging declared wars. Combatants have integrated themselves with noncombatants, and long-range weapons have downgraded both the potential and the value of sanctuaries from combat.

Note that the concern includes sensitivity not only for military casualties, but also enemy civilian casualties. The laws of armed conflict, covered in detail in Chapter 3, are straightforward on the matter of refraining from targeting noncombatants, and even if they are not targeted, on ensuring that they are protected. Perhaps the logical extreme was reached in the Clinton administration's 1994 cruise missile attack on Iraq in retaliation for the failed assassination plot against ex-President Bush. The launches were carried out against the Iraqi intelligence agency that planned the attempt. But they were executed at night, when the guilty parties were almost certain not to be in their offices.[44]

---

[41]Lawrence Freedman and Efraim Karsh, *The Gulf Conflict 1990-1991: Diplomacy and War in the New World Order* (Princeton, N.J.: Princeton University Press, 1993), 286.

[42]"The official US military casualty figures as of 24 June 1991 are as follows: killed in action—148; wounded in action—458; non-battle deaths—138; non-battle injuries—2978. . . . Estimates for non-US Coalition military casualties are: killed in action—192; wounded in action—318." United States, Office of the Secretary of Defense, *Conduct of the Persian Gulf Conflict: An Interim Report to Congress* (July 1991), 27-1.

[43]Jeffrey Record writes on this score, "Indeed, the evidence suggests that the desire to minimize both U.S. military and Iraqi civilian casualties was the single most important determinant of the shape and course of Desert Storm." *Hollow Victory: A Contrary View of the Gulf War* (Washington, D.C.: Brassey's (U.S.), Inc., 1993), 151.

[44]"Not only aversion to casualties, but also wars are required to be fought with 'a minimum number of casualties inflicted on the *enemy*.' " Walter J. Boyne, *Beyond the Wild Blue: A History of the Air Force 1947–1997*, 1997, 7. Quoted in Dunlap, *Technology*, 4.

The extent to which the operations over Kosovo in 1999 were conducted with great sensitivity to potential civilian casualties, and how this imposed operational constraints on the action, is clear in this statement by the U.S. Secretary of Defense:

> "Let me say for the record that most of you have no idea—nor should you—of the extraordinary effort in planning by the military leadership to make sure we minimized civilian casualties [in the operation over Kosovo, 1999]," Cohen said. "[The planners asked] what types of aircraft were used, under what circumstances, what type of munitions, what was the blast effect, what was the angle of attack. All of that was taken under consideration every single day of the 78-day campaign," Cohen said.[45]

Finally, on the issue of casualties, Michael Howard deserves the last word: "To put it in brutal terms, soldiers must not only know how to kill, but must also be prepared if necessary to die. More important, the societies that commit them to action must be prepared to see them die, and in these days of CNN quite literally so. Western societies have learned how to kill on an enormous scale, but they may still have to fight at a disadvantage against agrarian age armies who have not forgotten how to die and know well-enough how to kill."[46]

Quite appropriately, very high levels of concern attend the issue of causing casualties to one's own forces, called "amicicide,"[47] "fratricide," or "blue-on-blue" engagements. This gives rise to many operational constraints, one of the most confining of which is the necessity for positive identification of targets—which in many cases requires no less than visual sighting.[48] Obviously, the value of long-range weapons is severely diminished by such requirements.

---

[45]Jim Garamone, "Cohen Rejects Revisionists' Views of Kosovo Operation," *Defense Press Service,* <http://www.defenselink.mil/news/Feb2000/n02072000_20002073.html>, February 7, 2000.

[46]Michael Howard, "How Much Can Technology Change Warfare?" in *Two Historians in Technology and War,* Sir Michael Howard and John F. Guilmartin, Jr. (Carlisle Barracks, Pa.: U.S. Army War College, July 20, 1994), 8.

[47]See Charles R. Shrader, *Amicicide: The Problem of Friendly Fire in Modern War,* Combat Studies Institute Research Survey No. 1 (Ft. Leavenworth, Kans.: U.S. Army Command and General Staff College, 1982).

[48]See Guy R. Phillips, "Rules of Engagement: A Primer," *The Army Lawyer,* DA Pamphlet 27-50-248, July 1993, 4–27.

In the final analysis, the combination of all the constraints, risks, and levels of commitment have led, in the case of the action over the Balkans in 1999 and extending back to the Vietnam War, to target selection being made at very high levels in the U.S. government.[49] Sometimes referred to as the "three thousand mile screwdriver," this propensity has, if anything, increased as the ability to see the "common operational picture"—providing the same environment and prospectus from the tactical to the strategic levels—has increased by orders of magnitude in the information age.

Thus, it can be seen that operational constraints arising from the strategic defensive, the interaction of ends, ways, means, and risks, and reservations about the effects of the use of military force inhibit the employment of the U.S. military instrument. Some of the constraints are blatant, while others are quite subtle. All, because of the openness of U.S. society, are transparent to potential adversaries, setting the stage for asymmetrical approaches. All are real, however, and all are effective. Those effects will be analyzed in detail in Chapter 5.

---

[49]Indeed, "A Clinton aide told the *New York Times* that the president is personally giving clearance to the Pentagon on buildings hit in Belgrade, to make sure the targets are chosen with political sensitivity. The aide, evidently showcasing the president's skills as a warrior-diplomat, seems never to have heard of Lyndon Johnson. Johnson came to grief constantly reviewing target lists and making them conform to his political goals during the Vietnam War." Jim Hoagland, "Shades of LBJ," *Washington Post*, April 7, 1999, 21.

CHAPTER 2

Organizational Constraints

Against the possibility that the United States might somehow retain the means
with which to project power effectively, the administration is subordinating the
nation's freedom of action to myriad international arrangements. These include:
insisting on securing U.N. Security Council or other multilateral blessing prior to
U.S. use of force; agreeing to the Kyoto Climate Change protocol that explicitly
subjects any unilaterally mounted military operation or training activity to
greenhouse gas emission restrictions; embracing a Law of the Sea treaty that will
imperil, not protect American interests in freedom of navigation and use of
international waters; and proposing to allow U.S. servicemen and women to be
prosecuted by an unconstitutional International Criminal Court.

Frank Gaffney, Jr.

President Jacques Chirac said today that France had used its veto
power over proposed NATO targets in Yugoslavia to prevent the
alliance from bombing Belgrade's bridges. "Not a single air strike—and
there were about 22,000 of them—was carried out without France's
approval. . . . When France objected, the strikes were not carried
out," Chirac said on French television TF1.[1]

A second family of constraints on the use of force arises from the way
the U.S. government is organized and the way it chooses to structure the
conduct of military operations. A democratic form of government with
great skepticism about the use of force, separate war-making powers
located in different sectors of the government, civilian control of the
military, a free press, and an inclination to expand the use of force internationally to include friends and allies—all contribute to controlling
both the propensity to use force and its application.

A growing body of literature confirms the proposition that democracies tend to be peace seeking and peaceable. Democracies do not make

---

[1]"Chirac Says He Spared the Bridges," *Washington Post*, June 11, 1999, 17.

war on one another: "Never has there been a war involving violent military action between stable democracies."[2] While there has been a recent spate of these studies, their roots are deep. Over thirty years ago, in a widely acclaimed study of interstate warfare, Quincy Wright observed, "Absolutistic states with geographically and functionally centralized governments under autocratic leadership are likely to be most belligerent, whereas constitutional states with geographically and functionally federalized governments under democratic leadership are likely to be most peaceful."[3] Even earlier, "Alexis de Tocqueville made the point in all its baldness: 'Democratic nations naturally desire peace.' "[4]

Democracies find it difficult to deal with interstate violence, for "Democracies, with rare exceptions, always incline to pacifism, and they find it difficult to understand those who do not share this predisposition: how can anyone be so unreasonable as to consider war an instrument for the solution of conflicts?"[5]

As the agent of its citizens, democratic government looks initially toward domestic peace and prosperity. The vox populi acts as a tether and a brake on personal ambitions of elected leaders. Democracies are anti-imperialistic, and they follow international agendas that evince a preference for cooperation over conflict. They tend to favor international organizations to adjudicate state-to-state disagreements, whether they extend to disputes about commerce, territory, or international migration of people, animals, and pollution. Democratic forms of government limit the level and kinds of military actions undertaken by the representative military forces.[6] Thus, the very form of government exerts an organizational constraint on the use of military force.

---

[2]R. J. Rummel, *Death by Government* (New Brunswick, N.J.: Transaction Publishers, 1994), 2. See also Bruce Russett, *Grasping the Democratic Peace: Principles for a Post-Cold War World* (Princeton, N.J.: Princeton University Press, 1993) and Spencer Weart, "Why They Don't Fight: Democracies, Oligarchies, and Peace," *In Brief* 48 (Washington, D.C.: United States Institute of Peace, November 1993).

[3]Quincy Wright, *A Study of War*, abridged (Chicago: University of Chicago Press, 1964), 161–162.

[4]Quoted in Joffe, "Democracy and Deterrence," in Miller and Smith, *Ideas and Ideals* 114.

[5]Walter Laqueur, *The Political Psychology of Appeasement: Finlandization and Other Unpopular Essays* (New Brunswick, N.J.: Transaction Books, 1980), 135.

[6]Weart observes, "Not only modern democracies, but all democracies, have kept peace with one another." "Why They Don't Fight," 1.

The separation of powers in the United States and the constitutional assignment of different war-making responsibilities to the legislative and executive branches of the government provide another level of limitation on the use of force. Different executives and congresses have approached the questions raised by the exercise of war powers in manifestly different ways. Arguably, Franklin D. Roosevelt was among the most independent of presidents, for even though he was acting as commander-in-chief in a declared war, he "did not consult Congress about war aims, refused the legislators either a major presence or influence at the great war-time conferences that forged strategy, and even failed to provide Congress with much more information than it could glean from newspapers."[7] The relationship between the executive and legislative branches with regard to the authority to use military power evolved over the years, and was brought to a head by the passage in 1973 by the Congress—angry at the incursion into Cambodia during the Vietnam War and over the veto of President Nixon—of the War Powers Resolution.

The perverse way in which the American citizenry routinely elects legislatures and executives from different parties exacerbates the problem. The War Powers Resolution, for example, "is not a compromise between the two branches of government to allocate war powers. Rather, it was imposed on a hostile President by an equally hostile Congress."[8] Irrespective of the merits of the debate, which is unlikely to be resolved, the inevitable suspicion and resultant tension between the governmental branches forms a clear limitation on the use of force.[9]

---

[7]Eliot A. Cohen, "The Strategy of Innocence? The United States, 1920–1945," in *The Making of Strategy: Rulers, States and War*, Williamson Murray, MacGregor Knox, and Alvin Bernstein (New York: Cambridge University Press, 1994), 435–436.

[8]Robert D. Clark, Andrew M. Egeland, Jr., and David B. Sanford, *The War Powers Resolution* (Washington, D.C.: National War College, 1985), 19.

[9]"With respect to the use of force, it is a largely negative activism [within the U.S. Congress] that seeks to block or restrict the use of force on one ground or another. Examples of such congressional activism include the 1973 War Powers Act, the 1976 Clark Amendment (prohibiting any kind of U.S. assistance to Angola without congressional authorization), the 1993 Byrd Amendment (setting a deadline for withdrawal of U.S. forces from Somalia), the 1994 Helms Amendment (requiring prior congressional authorization for any use of force in Haiti), and the 1994 Dole Amendment (mandating a unilateral U.S. termination of the United Nations arms embargo of Bosnia)." Jeffrey Record, "Congress, Information Technology, and the Use of Force," in *The Information Age: An Anthology on Its Impact and Consequences*, David S. Alberts and Daniel S. Papp, ed. (Washington, D.C.: The Center for Advanced Concepts and Technologies, 1997).

The ability of the Congress to throttle funding for military activities in peacetime acts as another control on prospective uses of military power. Operations and maintenance funds support military operations by U.S. forces on a global scale. Reductions in those funds restrict available military options. Moreover, funding constraints might be seen by potential adversaries as asymmetrical opportunities—not only because of lower deployment levels of U.S. forces but also because they know that military operations are expensive, and cost is certainly an important consideration in the decision to apply the military instrument.[10]

A free, independent, burgeoning news media and the instantaneous transmission of information on a global basis also have a depressant effect on options to use force. The contemporary media tend to devalue intelligence sources, render information more perishable, enhance the short-term effects of deception and disinformation while probably reducing their long-term viability, reduce the time available for decision making, and bring the general public into all debates about the use of force. On occasion, other states have refused to share information with the United States because of their concern that secrets cannot be adequately safeguarded in such an open society. The U.S. Freedom of Information Act appears to raise eyebrows in this regard. With aggressive reporting threatening exposure, it is difficult to maintain secrecy, especially of an operation that requires significant movement of military forces. The rapid distribution and penetration of information today can increase the short-term impact of deception or psychological operations.[11] At the same time, the half-life of deceptive practices is probably lower, given the enhanced ability to expose them. Adversaries, recognizing that their intentions are more and more likely to be compromised, look at shorter and shorter timelines for action. Finally, decision makers must now, as never before, consider public reactions to their actions.

---

[10]This is not just a hypothetical concern. "An early 1993 newspaper article on President Bill Clinton's budget proposals noted that a military operation the size of Desert Storm can erase a year's worth of deficit improvement. U.S. political leaders may feel constrained by this consideration; our opponents may be more inclined to take risks." Commander C. P. Mott, U.S. Navy, "Naval Forces After . . . From the Sea," *United States Naval Institute Proceedings* (September 1993): 45.

[11]Psychological operations comprise a form of information operations in which information is disseminated purposefully to influence foreign audiences. Public affairs, in contrast, are not targeted specifically at external audiences.

The media opens for scrutiny the interworkings of the government and holds it to standards of justification for its policies and actions. It provides a window into the results of the use of force, causing reappraisals of actions and peremptory rejection of some courses of action. As Patrick Glynn has noted, there is now a "participatory universe," one that "tends to push national leaders, and especially American presidents, toward an increasing emphasis on humanitarian involvements and toward a minimization of violence."[12]

What has been dubbed "the CNN factor" can also be a "stampeding factor," causing decision makers to take decisions rapidly, and perhaps precipitately. The CNN factor contributes to the already high emphasis in today's military operations on speed and operational tempo. Still, the major impact of the media and public opinion has weighed in on the side of constraint. Robert Jervis offers this salient observation: "Perhaps the main inhibitor of the U.S. threat to punish others . . . is not retaliation by the adversary but rather the expected adverse response on the part of the world and U.S. public opinion."[13] Public opinion tends to influence not only whether military power will be used, but also its form, extent, and duration. The power of public opinion and its influence on policy has increased substantially since about 1970.

Civilian control of the military, a desirable feature deeply ingrained in U.S. strategic culture, might also be viewed as a constraint. Curiously, however, the general trend has been for the opposite to be the case. For more than twenty years, the record shows that "on the question of committing American troops abroad, the military generally have been more cautious than the president's most aggressive principal civilian advisers. . . . The leading hawks have been the civilian, not the military, advisers."[14] Once hostilities begin, on the other hand, "While politicians may be inclined to use limited force in hopes of

---

[12]Glynn, "Quantum Leap," 54.

[13]Robert Jervis, "What Do We Want to Deter and How Do We Deter It?" in *Turning Point: The Gulf War and U.S. Military Strategy*, ed. L. Benjamin Ederington and Michael J. Mazarr (Boulder, Colo.: Westview Press, 1994), 128.

[14]David H. Petraeus, "Military Influence and the Post-Vietnam Use of Force," *Armed Forces and Society* 15, 4 (Summer 1989): 490. See also David H. Petraeus, *The American Military and the Lessons of Vietnam* (Ann Arbor: University of Michigan Microfilms, 1987), and Bruce Berkowitz, "Introduction," in *The United States and the Use of Force in the Post-Cold War Era*, The Aspen Strategy Group (Queenstown, Md.: The Aspen Institute, 1995), xviii.

achieving a political settlement in the midst of calculated escalation, the military's agenda inevitably involves military victory in the swiftest, surest fashion possible."[15]

Civilian control grows out of a deep-seated concern on the part of U.S. citizens about the exercise of authority in general, and the central government in particular. The Constitution and Bill of Rights offer safeguards for civilian—and popular—control of the government. Yet, there are powerful lobbies and pockets of resistance in the United States seeking to constrain the ability of the state to exercise its authority. This is not unique to the United States, nor is it new. The Romans asked, *quis custodiet ipsos custodes?* (Who will guard the guards?)

This dichotomy between the civilian and military leadership has yet another dimension, a more subtle one. Reporting on a study conducted by the Triangle Institute of Security Studies, Don Snider remarked on the differences between veterans and nonveterans in political leadership positions in the United States. The issue of interest was the propensity to use force and how restraints were applied. According to the study, "The fewer the number of veterans, the more likely it was that force would be used, but that it would be used with restraint." This is in keeping with the military inclination to employ overwhelming effort once the decision has been taken to use force. Given the current and anticipated complexion of the U.S. legislative branch, in which military veterans will become fewer and farther between, Snider concludes that civil-military frictions will extend into the future, "which poses potential difficulties for alliance relationships and global leadership."[16]

An increased domestic focus by both the executive and legislative branches can be seen as an additional hobble on the use of force internationally. Arnold Kanter and Linton Brooks note that "the growing priority of domestic considerations makes both unilateral U.S. action and U.S. leadership of international coalitions more difficult politically."[17] Moreover, "Fears of the domestic political consequences of

---

[15]Jane E. Holl, "We the People Here Don't Want No War: Executive Branch Perspectives on the Use of Force," in Aspen, *United States Use of Force*, 129.

[16]Don M. Snider, "America's Postmodern Military," *World Policy Journal*, Spring 2000 [electronic version].

[17]Arnold Kanter and Linton F. Brooks, eds., *U.S. Intervention Policy for the Post-Cold War World: New Challenges and New Responses* (New York: W. W. Norton & Company, 1994), 23.

becoming involved in a real war work to restrain the belligerent actions of leaders."[18] The ordinary wisdom is that the American public is reluctant to fight, but, once aroused and engaged, believes in winning—as quickly and as effectively as possible. Public support for the operations in Afghanistan following the September 11, 2001, attacks confirmed this observation.

*Intra*state squabbles on the use of force notwithstanding, there is also a series of *inter*state hindrances. On the one hand, the multiplication of independent states over the past forty years and the end of the polarizing power of the Cold War offer a much larger matrix for involvement. On the other hand, virtually all states of the world are now members of the United Nations, a collective security organization. While international organizations provide some top cover for the use of force, they also bring their own set of constraints. Naturally, when the United States enters a coalition or alliance with others, it wants to impose on them its own ideas about the use of force. Just as naturally, its partners will want to impress their ideas on the United States. This means that adjustments and compromises must be made in any unilateral U.S. approach.

The United States has found it useful when applying force to do so under multilateral banners if at all possible. In some cases it has gone to great lengths to provide a multinational rationale for its actions— involvement of the Organization of Eastern Caribbean States (an organization not heard of before or since) in the Grenada operation of 1983 offering the exemplary nadir. In the 1991 Gulf War, the Bush administration sought to apply U.N. Security Council Resolution 678 calling for the use of "all means necessary" to enforce previous resolutions as an exemption to the War Powers Act on notification of the Congress on the use of the U.S. military. The net effect of "deference to supranational authority," however, has been to constrain "nation-states, even great powers, from acting in pursuit of their own immediate interests."[19] While the United States would prefer that others defer to its Great Power status, it recognizes at the same time that it must act with great circumspection.

---

[18]Bruce Russett, *Controlling the Sword: The Democratic Governance of National Security* (Cambridge, Mass.: Harvard University Press, 1990), 47.

[19]Andrew J. Bacevich, "The Limits of Orthodoxy: The Use of Force after the Cold War," in Aspen, *United States Use of Force*, 173.

Concurrent with the general reorientation of focus more toward domestic affairs, there has been a general implosion of U.S. military presence abroad. "Overseas bases symbolize U.S. interests and influence because, fundamentally, they are symbols of military power," wrote James Blaker. "As such," he continued, "bases derive their political impact from the way they can facilitate the use of U.S. military force."[20] From a post-World War II structure that included over 2,000 bases, in 1995 the United States operated its forces from 171 bases in 32 foreign states and territories.[21] This contraction in the number of overseas bases, which clearly has not reached its conclusion, acts as a constraint. For force even to be considered, it must be usable. If it is near the geographic point of application, its use is made easier. To travel long distances, particularly if long transit times and substantial logistic trains are involved, as is the case with large ground forces, for example, reduces both the opportunity and the inclination to use force.

Allies have constrained U.S. efforts on many occasions. For example, NATO allies would not permit the U.S. to overfly them in the Arab-Israeli Conflict of 1973, and overflight rights were not granted in the 1986 U.S. air strikes on Libya originating in the United Kingdom. In September 1996, when missile strikes were conducted against Iraq for its actions in the north against the Kurds, Jordan would not permit the U.S. air expeditionary force to return (exercises had been conducted in the spring) and Turkey refused the use of its Incirlik base.[22] More recently, "With Saudi Arabia showing deep reluctance to support a military strike on Iraq, Secretary of Defense William S. Cohen said today that he would not seek permission to launch American fighters and bombers from Saudi territory."[23]

An old saw inside the beltway in Washington, D.C. contends that the timing is never right for the State Department. "What do you mean you want to conduct military operations in Fredonia tomorrow? Don't

---

[20]James R. Blaker, *United States Overseas Basing: An Anatomy of the Dilemma* (New York: Praeger, 1990), 3.

[21]William R. Evinger, ed., *Directory of U.S. Military Bases Worldwide* (Phoenix, Ariz.: Oryx Press, 1995).

[22]John J. Fialka, "U.S. Is Stretched As Allies Lie Low over Iraq Attacks," *Wall Street Journal*, September 12, 1996, 1.

[23]Steven Lee Myers, "U.S. Will Not Ask to Use Saudi Bases for a Raid on Iraq," *New York Times*, February 9, 1998, 1. Secretary Cohen was attempting to build support for an attack on Iraq for failing to comply with U.N. inspection efforts.

you know that it's the birthday of the second cousin to the Queen of Danark? Do you want the Danarkis to be outraged?" parodies a typical Department of State cavil against this kind of approach. Almost as many, and as inventive, excuses were raised during the classic instance of organizational interference to the use of force by allies in the March–June 1999 bombing of Serbia and Kosovo. On the one hand, the allies declined to attack one of Slobodan Milosevic's residences because it contained a Rembrandt painting; in another instance, Italy asked for a bombing pause over Easter, in part because the war might scare away holiday tourists from Venice;[24] in still another, Pope John Paul II reportedly sent a request to NATO for a ten-day pause in bombing from Roman Catholic Good Friday through the Serbian Orthodox Easter Sunday;[25] and the French were even reluctant to attack radio and television outlets in Serbia because "the idea of killing journalists—well, we were very nervous about that."[26] The tight control stemmed from a perception that no participant in the NATO alliance could tolerate defeat—or even an expensive victory.[27] At one point in April 1999, it was reported that British Prime Minister Tony Blair came to General Wesley Clark's office when Clark was the officer in direct command of the NATO operation dubbed "Allied Force" in Serbia and Kosovo. The Prime Minister told General Clark "that the future of every leader in Europe depended on the outcome."[28]

In the United Nations, there is a layering effect on the use of force. The Security Council veto stands as the first barrier. Prospects of a Security Council veto led NATO to conduct its intervention in Kosovo

---

[24]Charles Krauthammer, "Bombing Empty Buildings," *Washington Post*, April 8, 1999, 31.

[25]Carla Anne Robbins, Thomas E. Ricks, and Neil King, Jr., "Milosevic's Resolve Spawned Unity, Wider Bombing List in NATO Alliance," *Wall Street Journal*, April 27, 1999, 1.

[26]Attributed to a "French diplomat." "Ralston Sees Potential for More Wars of Gradual Escalation," *Inside the Pentagon*, September 16, 1999, 1.

[27]"The arrival of body bags in Rome, Paris, Amsterdam, Prague, Budapest, and other capitals would precede by a few days, if not hours, serious anti-NATO demonstrations in these cities. Failure to anticipate the volatility of public opinion on the Continent could make the initial decision to launch missiles appear, by comparison, a paragon of military acumen. And NATO would suffer a huge setback should the profoundly troubled Operation Allied Force devolve into a protracted, bloody farce." George W. Grayson, "How to Wreck NATO: Launch a Ground War in the Balkans," *Christian Science Monitor*, April 28, 1999.

[28]Michael Ignatieff, "Annals of Diplomacy the Virtual Commander—How NATO Invented a New Kind of War," *New Yorker*, August 2, 1999 [electronic version].

essentially outside the U.N. framework. The U.N. veto will undoubtedly loom even larger as a peer competitor to the United States arrives on the scene or the Security Council is increased in size—both of which seem likely in the next decade or so. Although the United Nations is the parent organization for the bulk of worldwide peacekeeping efforts, it stands foursquare against intervention into the internal *and external* affairs of other states, providing those affairs are legitimately in keeping with the U.N. Charter.[29] A debate has been taking place about the legality of preventive or anticipatory self-defense under the terms of the Charter. One side of the debate argues that Article 51 of the Charter[30] rules out other than after-the-fact retaliation in self-defense, the other takes the position that preemptory actions are permitted—that one does not have to absorb the first blow. Yoram Dinstein, moreover, asserts, "The use of the phrase 'armed attack' in Article 51 is not inadvertent. . . . The choice of words in Article 51 is deliberately restrictive. The exercise of the right of self-defense, in conformity with the Article, is confined to a response to an armed attack."[31]

In Somalia, the United Nations exercised constraint on the ability of U.S. forces to operate independently. "The [Senate Armed Services Committee] report is based on a two-year study of the firefight in Mogadishu Oct. 3, 1993, and tells how top administration officials, including National Security Adviser Anthony Lake and Mr. Aspin [then-Secretary of Defense], allowed the United Nations to influence deployment of U.S. forces, with disastrous results."[32] Such conclusions notwithstanding, restraint and interference must be expected whenever

---

[29]UNGA 2131, 1965: "No state has right to intervene, directly or indirectly, with internal and external affairs of other states."

[30]Article 51: "Nothing in the present Charter shall impair the inherent right of individual or collective self-defence if an armed attack occurs against a Member of the United Nations, until the Security Council has taken measures necessary to maintain international peace and security. Measures taken by Members in the exercise of this right to self-defence shall be immediately reported to the Security Council and shall not in any way affect the authority and responsibility of the Security Council under the present Charter to take at any time such action as it deems necessary in order to maintain or restore international peace and security."

[31]Yoram Dinstein, *War, Aggression, and Self Defense*, 2nd ed. (Cambridge, U.K.: Grotius Publications, Cambridge University Press, 1994), 183. A discussion of "preemptive self defense" appears in this book at 128–129.

[32]Bill Gertz, "Aspin's Decision on Tanks Was Political," *Washington Times*, October 3, 1995, 3.

U.S. forces are operating under the guidance of or in concert with other international military forces.

Sometimes overt, sometimes latent, organizational structure makes an imprint on the ability of U.S. decision makers to use force on the international scene. The points of application of the restraints are varied but additive. Because they apply uniquely to the United States, they constitute another breeding ground for asymmetrical actions. Others—those who would oppose the United States—are neither ignorant nor indifferent to the constraints outlined here. Ultimately, organizational constraints combine with other forms of restraint to produce a range of effects, which will be entertained in Chapter 5.

CHAPTER 3

Legal Constraints

The 1899 Hague Conference was the first at which the Japanese were present as international equals of the European and American powers which had hitherto engrossed the making of international law. But by what title had Japan got there? "We show ourselves at least your equals in scientific butchery, and at once we are admitted to your council tables as civilized men."

Richard Best

History is written by the victors. Thus, the heinous massacre that was Hiroshima has been handed down to us as a perfectly justified act of war.

Takashi Hiraoka, Mayor of Hiroshima

Operational and organizational constraints on the use of force may or may not be underwritten in law. Beyond those particular constraints, however, a developed body of international law has evolved to confine the use of force in a variety of ways. The historical roots of this body of law lie with notions of chivalry on the battlefield, a belief that all human activity should be bounded by the rule of law, a Western revulsion at the results of the use of force in past conflicts, concern that force be used only as a last resort, and the idea that wars and their battles are to be fought by certain groups of people, while others are to be exempt from their ravages. The centerpiece of the legal approach is that the use of force and its effects should be confined, as much as possible, to combatants. No direct and intentional harm should be visited upon noncombatants when force is used. Closely associated with an approach that seeks to detail the laws of armed conflict are efforts in arms control: for what better way to ensure against the use of force than to remove weapons from the hands of those who might be tempted to use them?

The pertinent laws are wide-ranging and complex. They provide an ever-thickening web of restraint. Moreover, activists are vigilant and eager to increase the strands of the web and to free it of its imperfections. Their agenda states clearly:

> Any broadening of the interpretation of the right to resort to military force is fraught with danger. . . . Therefore international law must develop along the path of eliminating all loopholes in the legal regulation of the ban on the use of force. . . . Unilateral coercive military measures must disappear from international practice in the future. In this regard international law must become maximally clear and unambiguous in not permitting any broad interpretation of the right to rely on force.[1]

International law is both agreed and customary. In the former it appears as international treaties, protocols, conventions, opinions of international courts and tribunals, and other documents to which a state is a party. In the latter it

> derives from the practice of military and naval forces in the field, at sea, and in the air during hostilities. When such a practice attains a degree of regularity and is accompanied by the general conviction among nations that behavior in conformity with that practice is obligatory, it can be said to have become a rule of customary law *binding all nations*.[2]

It should be noted that a particular state need not agree with the particular tenet of customary law for it to be obligatory. It should also be noted that there is significant disagreement among nations as to what constitutes "the precise content of an accepted practice of armed conflict and to its status as a rule of law."[3] Moreover, both forms of international law involve relationships among sovereign states, not individuals or nonstate groups.

---

[1]Lori Fisler Damrosch and David J. Scheffer, eds., *Law and Force in the New International Order* (Boulder, Colo.: Westview Press, 1991), 20.

[2]Department of the Navy, Office of the Chief of Naval Operations, *The Commander's Handbook on the Law of Naval Operations* NWP 1-14M, 5-2. Emphasis added.

[3]Ibid., 5–3.

In the United States, all weapons under development must undergo a legal review,[4] as must the development of tactics, techniques, capabilities, and rules of engagement. All members of the U.S. armed services are required to be trained in the principles and rules of the law of war, the responsibility for which is assigned to the secretaries of the military departments.[5]

Despite an extended evolution, the law of armed conflict contains areas of disagreement and, regardless of efforts to eliminate it, permits a range of interpretation. Moreover, its application and enforcement have been uneven. Some states in the international system have chosen to comply, while others have flouted their international responsibility to uphold the laws. Responses to noncompliance have been anything but consistent:

> When the Israelis bombed the Iraqi pre-operational nuclear reactor near Baghdad in 1981, world condemnation was rampant. Yet when the Coalition forces undertook precisely the same type of missions during the Gulf War, applause followed. When Argentina moved on the Falklands pointing to historical rationales over a century old, the act was not labeled aggression by the United Nations. When Iraqi forces invaded Kuwait citing twentieth century history and anticolonial motives, the United Nations not only branded the action aggression, but authorized the use of force to expel them. The world community accepted Tanzania's 1979 overthrow of Idi Amin's dictatorship in Uganda, but criticized Viet Nam's unseating of the at least as bloody Pol Pot regime the same year. The 1979 Soviet invasion of neighboring Afghanistan resulted in United Nations calls for withdrawal; four years later when the United States invaded Grenada, the United Nations remained silent.[6]

---

[4]"The U.S. military has carried out legal reviews on its weapons systems since 1974, after many of the weapons it used in Vietnam were challenged under international law. . . . The United States is a leader in reviewing its own systems for compliance with international law. Although there is an international treaty signed by 155 nations calling for internal legal review, only about a dozen nations actually perform them." David Atkinson, "New Weapons Technologies Offer Complex Issues for Review," *Defense Daily*, September 1, 1999, 2.

[5]DoD Directive 5100.77, July 10, 1979.

[6]Major Michael N. Schmitt, USAF, "The Resort to Force in International Law: Reflections on Positivist and Contextual Approaches," *Air Force Law Review* 37, 105 (1994): 113–114. This excellent article contains an extended review of the issues.

The law is grounded in just war theory, which is bifurcated into *jus ad bellum* and *jus in bello*. The former deals with questions having to do with the right to make war, while the latter is concerned with the conduct of war.

Jus ad Bellum

Thomas Aquinas argued that three tests were necessary to justify the use of force, *jus ad bellum*. The first, *just cause*, contended that the use of force must originate in a sound legal basis, either natural law or the law of nations. The purpose for this grounding was to put the use of force on a more rational basis than, for example, religious or ideological wars. The second, *competent authority*, meant that wars could be waged only by the initiation or with the consent of rulers. Ordinary citizens or nonauthoritative groups could not meet this test for *jus ad bellum*. The third, *right intention*, meant that conquest or wanton destruction, for example, could not be justification for war making. The intention of the user of military force must be more noble and selfless. Justification for most asymmetrical uses of force—especially terrorism—would likely be trumped by all three tests.

Given this framework, the decision to make war was one that the sovereign was competent to make: the inherent right to wage war was one of the central tenets of sovereignty. "Since the end of the First World War," however, "we have witnessed a major departure from 'the sovereign right' idea and a return to a severely restricted legal right of States to resort to war."[7] In fact, today, *jus ad bellum* has been restricted exclusively to self-defense against armed aggression.[8] The Thomist tests: just cause, competent authority, and right intention have been narrowed to conform to the U.N. Charter's inherent right of self-defense, and nothing more. This constitutes one "right to rely on force" in the view of contemporary activists. A second, recent instance is that of "humanitarian intervention," such as was used in NATO's Kosovo

---

[7]G.I.A.D. Draper, "Wars of National Liberation and War Criminality," in Howard, *Restraints on War*, 137.

[8]"Nothing in the present Charter shall impair the inherent right of individual or collective self-defense if an armed attack occurs against a Member of the United Nations, until the Security Council has taken measures necessary to maintain international peace and security." *U.N. Charter*, Article 51.

action, Operation Allied Force, in 1999. The use of force in this case was not sanctioned by the United Nations, and in view of the Security Council veto, is unlikely to garner U.N. approval in the future. The tension arises from the incompatibility of humanitarian intervention and the principle of noninterference with the internal affairs of sovereign states, which is prohibited by the Charter.[9]

The universality of the United Nations—in which only Taiwan is the only major state that is not a member, and its status as an independent state de facto is in question—has effectively answered the Thomist agenda: just cause is only in self-defense, competent authority is only the attacked state or the United Nations acting in a collective defense, and right intention is only to redress the aggression that provided the just cause.

Yet, ambiguities persist despite such apparent pat answers. The United States, for example, has consistently reserved the right to act in anticipation of an attack. The U.S. argument hinges on the claim that it is not necessary, given the devastating impact of modern weapons, to absorb the first blow. One can conduct, in this view, "anticipatory self-defense," by striking an adversary that is preparing an attack. Agreement on this approach is far from universal, however. The U.N. Charter, considering only state actors, is also focused on an "armed attack." But that omits other methods of conducting warfare or most asymmetrical uses of force, such as terrorist attacks, computer hacking, or hostage taking, for example.

Jus ad bellum also contained prudential tests, ones that have applicability when self-defense under the terms of the U.N. Charter is contemplated. Those tests were: that the use of force would result in a preponderance of good over evil, that force would be used only as a last resort, that there would be a reasonable chance of success, and that peace be the expected outcome.

The first prudential test, the preponderance of good over evil, is also called the *proportionality of ends* test. It argues that the good ends served

---

[9]"Nothing contained in the present Charter shall authorize the United Nations to intervene in matters which are essentially within the domestic jurisdiction of any state or shall require the Members to submit such matters to settlement under the present Charter; but this principle shall not prejudice the application of enforcement measures under Chapter VII." *U.N. Charter*, Article 2(7).

must not be outweighed by the harm caused by the application of force. In the Gulf War, for example, in applying this test, "Some targets were specifically avoided because the value of destruction of each target was outweighed by the potential risk to nearby civilians or, as in the case of certain archaeological and religious sites, to civilian objects."[10] It is clear that this test is one that military commanders ponder continually when they use force.[11]

Directed against unnecessary suffering or superfluous injury, and based on Protocol I Additional to the Geneva Conventions of 1949, the principle of proportionality has a more tightly focused meaning than might be expected. The proportionality rule prohibits attacks that "may be expected to cause incidental loss of civilian life, injury to civilians, damage to civilian objects, or a combination thereof, which would be excessive in relation to the concrete and direct military advantage anticipated."[12] Given this definition, if Saddam Hussein had attacked the coalition forces in the Gulf War with chemical weapons, it would have likely been deemed disproportionate to have responded with a nuclear weapon. But, viewed on a larger scale than the "direct military advantage anticipated," might a nuclear response have caused other owners of chemical weapons to reevaluate their need for them? What if, given the U.S. nuclear response to a chemical attack, many—or even all—others who possessed chemical weapons decided that they were not worth having? If, on a scale larger than the "direct military advantage anticipated," the prospects for the future employment of chemical weapons were substantially reduced, or perhaps even eliminated, might that provide a strong challenge to the narrow view of proportionality? On a less majestic scale, if the use of nuclear weapons by the United States had caused Saddam Hussein to sue immediately for peace, to quit

---

[10]United States, Office of the Secretary of Defense, *Conduct of the Persian Gulf War: Final Report to Congress*, April 1992, O-10.

[11]As another example: "According to a classified report now being prepared by the Air Force, not only did the air campaign conducted against Serbian emplacements in Bosnia last year destroy approximately 60 percent of the targets identified—about a 10 percent improvement over the Desert Storm campaign—it did so with no collateral damage." "NATO Air Forces Inflicted No Collateral Damage in Bosnian Air Campaign," *Inside the Air Force*, July 19, 1996, 1.

[12]*Protocol Additional to the Geneva Conventions of 12 August 1949, and relating to the Protection of Victims of International Armed Conflicts* (Protocol I), Article 57, Para. 2(a)(iii).

Kuwait, and to come to terms, should that necessarily have been deemed "disproportionate"?[13]

The "last resort," or *ultima ratio*, test suggests that all other means to resolve the issue must be judged as ineffective before force can be used. Contrary to contemporary belief, there is no requirement to try other means first: diplomacy or trade policy, for example. Moreover, the test is one that is answered by logical, not by chronological ordering. Force might in fact be the first means employed by one who is convinced that no other method has a chance of being effective, and that time is of the essence. This is an important distinction: "last resort" does not equate to the exhaustion of all other means first. It implies that all others have been considered and rejected for good and sufficient reason. Nevertheless, this distinction goes unappreciated fully—or is ignored—by those who argue that last resort means that all other means must be exhausted first.

The third test is that the undertaking have a reasonable prospect of success. This would appear to mean that there should be no gambling and no high risks assumed, and, if defeat looks certain, the correct choice would be to surrender. The requirement is not so stringent, however. In some cases, one has few options and is obliged to fight even against long odds. Yet, the constraint is tangible: "The reasonable likelihood of success is a *sine qua non* of *jus ad bellum*. Human life is not to be hazarded lightly."[14]

The final test advises that, among a large agenda of potential ends, peace must be the one sought. Once again, there is latitude for interpretation here, beginning with the definition of the word "peace". Still, it is a test and a goal of *jus ad bellum*.

In summary, considerations of the initial use of force are fundamentally constrained by the U.N. Charter and, at a greater level of specificity, by the four prudential tests. States that care deeply about international order will regulate their behavior to conform with these

---

[13]The report of the Persian Gulf War contains a passage that veers away from this "direct military advantage" test. It says, "It [proportionality] prohibits military action in which the negative effects (such as collateral civilian casualties) clearly outweigh the military gain. This balancing may be done on a target-by-target basis, as frequently was the case during Operation Desert Storm, but also may be weighed in overall terms against campaign objectives." Department of Defense, *Conduct of the Persian Gulf War*, O-10.

[14]Seabury and Codevilla, *War*, 220.

constraints, or at a minimum, seek to justify their behavior within their terms. Actors that have less of a stake in international order or justice will not be so constrained, will feel less need for justification, and might just view these constraints as points of weakness to be taken advantage of with asymmetrical acts.

Jus in Bello

Once war has begun, whether or not it is being waged in accordance with the tests of *jus ad bellum*, its conduct comes under the provisions of *jus in bello*. War, under this doctrine, cannot be waged indiscriminately or disproportionately. Those are the two principles governing *jus in bello*.[15]

Discrimination in war means that noncombatants cannot be attacked directly and deliberately. Since this is the case, a corollary would imply that military targets must not be located near obvious civilian and humanitarian structures—hospitals, historical monuments, and the like. Measures such as economic blockades, under this rubric, tend to be controversial.[16] If belligerents do not discriminate among combatants and noncombatants, they would seem to be in violation of the principle of discrimination. This, and other humanitarian considerations, explains why the economic sanctions imposed on Iraq by the United Nations in August of 1990 exempted medical supplies and certain foodstuffs.

If civilians cannot be deliberately attacked, how can one account for the large number of civilian casualties in Germany and Japan in the Second World War? Jointly with its European allies the United States killed over 300,000 German civilians and, independently, a like number of Japanese civilians. Don't these constitute violations of the proscription on attacking civilians? Insofar as they resulted from targeting noncombatants, they clearly do.[17]

---

[15]They are characterized slightly differently in the "General Principles of the Law of Armed Conflict" contained in the *Commander's Handbook on the Law of Naval Operations*, to wit: "1. Only that degree and kind of force, not otherwise prohibited by the law of armed conflict, required for the partial or complete submission of the enemy with a minimum expenditure of time, life, and physical resources may be applied. 2. The employment of any kind or degree of force not required for the purpose of the partial or complete submission of the enemy with a minimum expenditure of time, life, and physical resources, is prohibited. 3. Dishonorable (treacherous) means, dishonorable expedients, and dishonorable conduct during armed conflict are forbidden." *NWP 1-14M*, 5-4 to 5-6.

[16]See, for example, the discussion in *NWP 1-14M*, page 8-4, footnote 15.

[17]At the time, these attacks were justified as reprisals. Such attacks are now prohibited under Geneva Additional Protocol I (1977) Article 51 (6).

In fact, during this century the proportion of civilian casualties imposed by armed conflict has increased from 1.5 percent in World War I to 90 percent in the 1980s.[18] However, the number of noncombatant deaths in wartime pales in comparison to the staggering totals of citizens who have been murdered by their own governments.

> Perhaps 35 million people, of whom 25 million were civilians, have died as a direct consequence of military operations since 1900. . . . During the same period, however, at least 100 million human beings have been killed by police forces or their equivalent, almost never using heavy weapons but relying on hunger, exposure, barbed wire, and forced labor to kill the bulk, executing the rest by shooting them with small arms, by rolling over them with trucks (a favorite technique in China around 1950), by gassing them, or, as in the Cambodian holocaust of 1975–79, by smashing their skulls with wooden clubs.[19]

In time of war, however, the only justification that can condone attacks that jeopardize noncombatants is covered by the principle of "military necessity," which permits belligerents to apply force as required to achieve legitimate military objectives. Peacetime wanton killing can claim no such justification.

Nevertheless, "the effort, central to the laws of war to discriminate between the soldier and the civilian is full of moral ambiguity as well as practical difficulty."[20] Indeed, this is merely another case in which choices must be made and decisions taken based on incomplete—sometimes even false—information, and the consequences will be hotly debated, whichever way they turn out.

The principle of military necessity states that "only that degree and kind of force, not otherwise prohibited by the law of armed conflict, required for the partial or complete submission of the enemy with a minimum expenditure of time, life, and physical resources may be applied."[21]

---

[18]Robert O. Muller, "Introduction," in Prokosch, Technology of Killing, ix.

[19]Seabury and Codevilla, War, 6-7. See also Rummel, Death by Government.

[20]Adam Roberts, "International Law and the Use of Force: Paper I," in New Dimensions in International Security, Part II, Adelphi Papers #266 (London: Published by Brassey's for the IISS, Winter 1991–1992), 63.

[21]NWP 1-14 M, p. 6-6.

Rather than a justification for the use of force where it might otherwise be proscribed, *The Commander's Handbook on the Law of Naval Operations* describes this as a "*restraint* designed to limit the application of force in armed conflict to that which is in fact required to carry out a lawful military purpose."[22] The concept of military necessity, however, like so many others in the legal field, is open to subjective judgment and debate. One man's military necessity might be viewed as another's brutal crime.

If noncombatants cannot be deliberately attacked, what about mutual assured destruction, the doctrine of the superpowers during the Cold War, under which they held each other's civilian population hostage against aggression? Adam Roberts lends some insight:

> Threatening the use of weapons or methods of warfare that would violate the traditional laws of war was seen as justified *if such threats prevented war altogether.* In particular, threats against cities or against centers of government, though they might be doubtful in laws-of-war terms, were perceived as offering a better basis for strategic stability than counter-force threats, with their notorious effects on strategic stability whether in peacetime or during crises.[23]

But the matter does not end there. Some believe that regardless of the ends (no war) the ways (threatening megadeaths of civilians) were still immoral. Paul Ramsey argues in this regard, "Whatever is wrong to do is wrong also to threaten, if the latter means 'mean to do.' If aiming indiscriminately in actual acts of war (or in fight-the-war policies) is wrong, so also is threatening indiscriminately aimed action wrong to adopt in deter-the-war policies. . . . To put the point bluntly, if counter-population warfare is murder, then counter-population deterrent threats are murderous."[24] Yet, Robert Pape counters by claiming that nuclear coercion relies on threats to noncombatants: "[T]he threat to civilians implied by any use of nuclear weapons is likely to overwhelm

---

[22]Ibid. Emphasis in the original.

[23]Roberts, "International Law," 55. Emphasis added.

[24]Paul Ramsey, "A Political Ethics Context for Strategic Thinking," in Kaplan, *Strategic Thinking*, 134–135.

their military impact. Accordingly, successful nuclear coercion rests on threats to civilians rather than against military vulnerabilities."[25]

The Vietnam War taught the United States that determining who was a civilian—and, accordingly, entitled to protection—and who was a combatant was not a simple matter. Deception operations by an adversary might also put noncombatants at risk. As James Turner Johnson notes, "This is the problem posed by Mao's dictum that guerillas should live among the populace like fish in the sea, and it is the problem posed by the PLO's habit of basing itself in the midst of civilian settlements."[26] But, deception is not invariably acceptable. There are perfidious means of deception that are patently impermissible, such as the improper use of a white flag of truce. Thus, Professor Johnson continues: "I believe that all these cases involve impermissible deception, and while there may be other variations of this practice, its distinguishing characteristic remains the obscuring of conditions that impose moral restraints on the use of force. Other forms of deception that do not undermine these restraints are permissible."[27]

Discriminating among combatants and noncombatants, never easy, is becoming more and more difficult over time.[28] Information warfare and space warfare are two new realms in which distinguishing between legitimate and illegitimate targets is becoming more and more difficult. The limiting case of determining who are and who are not combatants resides with terrorism. It lends a fine point to the question of the ends being insufficient to justify the means, for terrorism pivots on indiscriminate, unlawful targeting of innocents in order to influence the policies of others. Western legal tradition totally rules out terrorism, arguing that "if the only means at his disposal are the intentional harming of innocents . . . he must not fight."[29]

---

[25] Robert A. Pape, *Bombing to Win: Air Power and Coercion in War* (Ithaca, N.Y.: Cornell University Press, 1996), 10–11.

[26] James Turner Johnson, "Just War Tradition and Low-Intensity Conflict," in *International Law Studies 1995: Legal and Moral Constraints on Low-Intensity Conflict,* vol. 67, ed. Alberto R. Coll, James S. Ord, and Stephen A. Rose (Newport, R.I.: Naval War College, 1995), 167.

[27] Ibid.

[28] Colonel Charles J. Dunlap, Jr., has published a provocative article that opens challenges to the traditional considerations regarding noncombatants. See his "The End of Innocence: Rethinking Noncombatancy in the Post-Kosovo Era," *Strategic Review,* Summer 2000, 9–17.

[29] Seabury and Codevilla, *War,* 229.

Discrimination means also that collateral damage must be avoided to the extent possible in the conduct of military operations. This also is not as simple as it might seem:

> In each case, the extent of danger to the civilian population varies. It varies with the type of military objective attacked, the type of terrain, the type of weapons used, the kind of weather, and whether civilians are nearby. It also depends on the combatant's ability and mastery of bombardment techniques, the level of the conflict, and the type of resistance encountered during the attack.[30]

Disagreements rage on this issue every time military actions take place. In the Kosovo bombing, for example, "After a six-month investigation, including three weeks interviewing witnesses in Kosovo, the Human Rights Watch team determined that one-third of the number of lethal episodes and half the casualties could have been avoided if NATO nation forces had strictly followed the rules."[31] Yet, "[i]n practice, only 20 of the approximately 23,000 munitions expended by NATO in the 1999 Balkan air operations caused collateral damage or civilian casualties."[32] The subject of collateral damage is a vexing one; it can be determined neither unilaterally nor straightforwardly.

Proportionality as a principle of *jus in bello* argues that the costs of using force be warranted by the benefits obtained. It cautions against gratuitous or otherwise unnecessary harm and champions a minimum expenditure of time and assets to achieve one's objectives. Like discrimination, it requires some interpretation.

Proportionality does not imply "tit-for-tat." To respond to a single attack with three is not necessarily disproportionate. A proportionate attack might be described as what it takes to do the job, and

---

[30]United States, Department of the Air Force, *An Introduction to Air Force Targeting*, AFP 200-17, (June 23, 1989), 37.

[31]Elizabeth Becker, "Rights Group Says NATO Killed 500 Civilians in Kosovo War," *New York Times*, February 7, 2000.

[32]John A. Tirpak, "The State of Precision Engagement," *Air Force Magazine*, March 2000.

no more. Proportionality does not require, even though it implies, balance or equality. The more unequal the response, either in the means used or in the intensity, however, the more difficult proportionality is either to determine or to assess. The U.S. air campaign in the Gulf War, for example, was labeled "illegally disproportionate," by at least one observer.[33]

On the face of it, the principle of proportionality seems to violate sound military practice. That is, should not the military commander prefer to win 25–0 rather than 14–12? Must one necessarily assume risks and casualties in order to comply with the requirements of proportionality? How great must those risks and casualties be? Yet, just as one would not employ a nuclear response to a minor conventional attack or destroy the entire adversary air force for a single attack on a warship, there are boundaries of proportionality, even if they tend to exist only in the eye of the beholder.

Another difficulty with proportionality arises from deterrence doctrine. Deterrence is said to work because a prospective aggressor calculates that his gains would not be worth the costs incurred. Does this not imply that the response he is encouraged to anticipate, the one that deters his acts, will be disproportionate? Logically, would not a credible disproportionate threat deter more reliably than a proportionate one? On the side of the deterrer, does it not encourage the issuance of disproportionate threats? One is reminded of Paul Ramsey's assertion quoted earlier: "Whatever is wrong to do is wrong also to threaten, if the latter means 'mean to do.' "[34] But is not the essential ingredient of deterrence the credibility factor—the "mean to do"?[35] All such questions must remain open, but all exert their asymmetrical constraints on the use of force.

---

[33]See Bruce Ross, "The Case for Targeting Leadership in War," *Naval War College Review* (Winter 1993): 83.

[34]Ramsey, "Political Ethics," in Kaplan, *Strategic Thinking*, 134–135.

[35]In the seminal work on nuclear calculus, Herman Kahn posited: "If we want to have our strategic forces contribute to the deterrence of provocation, it must be credible. . . . Usually the most convincing way to look willing is to be willing." *On Thermonuclear War* (Princeton, N.J.: Princeton University Press, 1960), 287.

Law of Armed Conflict

The philosophical restraints of *jus ad bellum* and *jus in bello* have been cod-
ified and made more specific through a series of international agreements.
With regard to the subject at hand, the use of force, the following are the
most pertinent:

- 1907 Hague Convention[36]

   IV: Respecting the Laws and Customs of War on Land
   V: Respecting the Rights and Duties of Neutral Powers and Persons
   in Case of war on Land
   IX: Concerning Bombardment by Naval Forces in Time of War

- 1948 Convention on the Prevention and Punishment of the Crime
   of Genocide

- 1949 Geneva Conventions

- 1954 Hague Convention for the Protection of Cultural Property in
   the Event of Armed Conflict (United States is not a party and is not
   bound)

International agreements such as these serve to make explicit the
general arguments set forth earlier about the use of force. The Geneva
Conventions alone contain over four hundred detailed articles. The
Annex to Hague IV, Article 25, for example, holds that "The attack or
bombardment, by whatever means of towns, villages, dwellings, or
buildings which are undefended is prohibited." This is clearly in keeping with the idea of protecting noncombatants and ensuring that unnecessary suffering and wanton destruction of property are avoided. Under
the guidelines of military necessity, military objectives within towns can
be attacked, with assurances that collateral damage not be excessive.
Likewise, there is a prohibition on bombardment for the purpose of ter-
rorizing the civilian population.

Medical facilities are specifically exempted from bombardment, as are
buildings devoted to religion and the arts and historic monuments. Moreover, dams and other man-made restraints to floodwaters are protected if

---

[36]Hague III, Relative to the Opening of Hostilities, was rendered moot by the U.N. Charter.

the potential for harm to noncombatants would be proportionally exces-sive. Of course, the misuse of such places for military purposes relieves them of their protected status during the period of misuse. The Hague pro-visions also contain restrictions on the employment of naval mines.

In addition, there are restraints on assassination. Hague IV "is con-strued as prohibiting assassination, proscription or outlawry of an enemy, or putting a price on an enemy's head, as well as offering a reward for an enemy 'dead or alive.' "[37] As a matter of U.S. national policy, assassina-tion is forbidden by Executive Order 12333, but it is said *not* to apply in time of war, the distinction being made between assassination and tar-geting a state's wartime leaders.[38]

In view of these constraints, the widespread coalition attacks on the Iraqi civilian infrastructure in the Gulf War were challenged:

> Electrical supply; civil communications; oil supply, storage, and refin-ing; transportation means; and general governmental activity throughout the country were bombed. . . . But while the choice of the classes of these targets may not be in dispute, the necessity for attacking them, in terms of achieving the specific objectives of this war, and given its postulated duration, remains unclear.[39]

In addition, there has been a recent effort to render unlawful *any* use of nuclear weapons. Before the International Court of Justice,

> Countries arguing for the ban offered evidence of the horrors that nuclear weapons inflict. They said such weapons must be declared ille-gal because they violate the law of warfare as well as a host of human rights and environmental treaties. Countries with nuclear arms replied that their weapons are not inherently illegal and that their use may be banned only through negotiation—as with the conventions prohibit-ing chemical and biological weapons—and not by judicial order.[40]

---

[37]Ross, "Case for Targeting Leadership," 80.

[38]Ibid., 82.

[39]William M. Arkin, Damian Durrant, and Marianne Cherni, *On Impact: Modern Warfare and the Environment. A Case Study of the Gulf War* (London: Greenpeace, May 1991), 74.

[40]Stephen Kinzer, "Word for Word/Anti-Nuclear Reaction; Refusing to Learn to Love the Bomb: Nations Take Their Case to Court," *New York Times*, January 14, 1996 [Lexis-Nexis (April 15, 1997)].

The Court delivered its advisory opinion at the request of the General Assembly of the United Nations. In that opinion (which is not binding, unlike the judgments delivered by the Court in its ordinary jurisdiction) the court stated that "the threat or use of nuclear weapons would generally be contrary to the rules of international law applicable in armed conflict."[41] Yet, the court qualified its advice by admitting that it "cannot reach a definitive conclusion as to the legality or illegality of the use of nuclear weapons by a State in an extreme circumstance of self-defense, in which its very survival would be at stake."[42]

U.S. military forces are guided in their conduct regarding the use of force by rules of engagement, or ROE. ROE are promulgated by commanders to their subordinates in order to establish a framework under which the use of force might be initiated or prolonged. ROE exist at the national level, disseminated by the National Command Authority, and at each command level down to the tactical level. They provide means of additional control on the military actions of subordinate levels of command. Commanders can use ROE to fine-tune the actions of their subordinates in order to confine conflict to certain levels, geographic areas, or targets. ROE are "consistent with the law of armed conflict. . . . [and] often restrict combat operations far more than do the requirements of international law."[43] The inherent right of self-defense is strongly emphasized in U.S. rules of engagement. It should be noted that in multinational situations the ROE of participating states might differ, and the differences might be very radical. The degree of respect accorded to the ROE of others is a matter of command relationships and negotiations among the participating states and constitutes an organizational constraint on the use of force.

Still, any use of force tends to have a political base, whether it is conducted by the rules or not. In the Vietnam War, for example,

[i]n those instances in which U.S. attacks inadvertently hit prohibited targets, North Vietnam won the propaganda battle. International and

---

[41]Jennifer Scott, "World Court Says Nuclear Arms Illegal in War, But . . .," *Reuters,* July 8, 1996 [Lexis/Nexis (April 15, 1997)].

[42]International Court of Justice, *Legality of the Threat or Use of Nuclear Weapons,* Advisory Opinion, July 8, 1996, Paragraph 96, <http://www.://www.peacenet.org.disarm/icjtxt.html> (April 13, 1997).

[43]NWP 1-14M, 4-5.

American public opinion turned against the U.S. military by alleging
that illegal American air strikes caused the damage, notwithstanding
the fact that American air combat operations intentionally attacked
only legitimate targets under strict rules of engagement.[44]

Thus, even ROE tend to be politically—and legally—rather than operationally based.

Finally, the prospect of being held accountable for "war crimes" casts
a pall over considerations of the use of force. "The Nuremberg trials,"
wrote Bradd Hayes, "did underscore that military commanders have few,
if any, defenses for carrying out illegal acts. . . . The principle of holding military commanders responsible for implementing illegal orders has
a long history in United States law."[45] Criminal responsibility for violations of the law of war rests with those who order offenses committed or
who "[k]new or should have known of the offense(s), had the means to
prevent or halt them, and failed to do all which he was capable of doing
to prevent the offenses or their recurrence."[46] The defense of superior
orders—"I was only following the orders of my superior"—has long been
disallowed. So, military personnel have an obligation *not* to follow illegal
orders of superiors, and they are responsible both for knowledge of illegal
acts and those they *should have known about.* In an age where modern
weapons permit launching an attack from a room in an air-conditioned
building—or a ship or aircraft—thousands of miles away from its target,
without seeing, or in any other way sensing, the target, these standards
constitute a significant depressant to the legitimate use of force—one
that will exert greater and greater leverage over time. Ultimately, they
appear either to require long-range weaponeers not to launch their
weapons in the absence of full knowledge of their targets; or, alternatively, they will be totally ignored and ineffective. Ignored and ineffective except, of course, when the victors impose them at the postwar war
crime trials. It goes without saying that those who undertake asymmetrical acts of violence will be unaffected by such niceties.

---

[44]John G. Humphries, "Operations Law and the Rules of Engagement," *Airpower Journal* (Fall
1992): 34.

[45]Bradd C. Hayes, *Toward a Doctrine of Constraint,* Strategic Research Department Strategic Memorandum no. 9-94 (Newport, R.I.: Naval War College, 1994), 15.

[46]DoD, *Conduct of the Persian Gulf War,* O-25.

Arms Control

Provisions in international law for the purpose of regulating conduct constitute one approach to controlling the use of armed force. Another is to impose direct constraints on the weapons and weapon systems themselves. Organized efforts to take weapons out of the hands of people in order to control their use extend back at least as far as the denunciation by the Church of the "homicidal and heinous use of catapults" in 1139.[47] The Hague Conferences of 1899 and 1907 represented the first formal multinational attempt to outlaw certain kinds of weapons.

Until 1987, it could be cogently argued that arms control had never succeeded in more than formalizing and sanctifying the status quo. Arms control agreements merely ratified or extended the current state of affairs: The Outer Space Treaty of 1967 (Treaty on Principles Governing the Activities of States in the Exploration and Use of Outer Space, including the Moon and Other Celestial Bodies), or the Limited Test Ban of 1963 (Treaty Banning Nuclear Weapon Tests in the Atmosphere, in Outer Space and under Water), for example.

Or they gave legal voice to what states had no intention of doing anyway:

- The Seabeds Treaty of 1971 (Treaty on the Prohibition of the Emplacement of Nuclear Weapons and Other Weapons of Mass Destruction on the Sea-Bed and the Ocean Floor and in the Subsoil Thereof), or the

- 1972 Bacteriological Weapons Convention (Convention on the Prohibition of the Development, Production, and Stockpiling of Bacteriological (Biological) and Toxin Weapons and on Their Destruction).

The year 1987 marked a watershed because, in this year, the Intermediate Nuclear Forces (INF) Treaty (Treaty between the United States and the Soviet Union on the Elimination of Their Intermediate-Range and Shorter-Range Missiles) accomplished what others had been unable to do: to alter the status quo, and to effect actual negotiated reductions in weapon systems.

---

[47]Sandoz, "Preface," in Prokosch, *Technology of Killing*, xiii.

Among its many goals, arms control has sought to reduce the risk of war, constrain arms competition (called "arms races" by the champions of arms control),[48] reduce unnecessary suffering, and depress the effects of military spending. It includes quantitative and qualitative measures, geographic controls, communications and administrative pacts, and confidence-building measures—often in combination. From the Declaration Respecting Expanding Bullets (known as the Dum Dum Declaration) by the Hague Convention of 1899, through the so-called "Inhumane Weapons Convention" (Convention on Prohibitions or Restrictions on the Use of Certain Conventional Weapons which May be Deemed to be Excessively Injurious or to Have Indiscriminate Effects 1981) to the Chemical Weapons Convention, effective in 1997, arms control has sought in a myriad of ways to restrain the use of force. Most recently, land mines, laser weapons, child soldiers, and even small arms have been the focus of attention of arms control.

While great amounts of energy have been devoted to the pursuit of arms control, its effects have been mixed. According to Louis Halle, in words penned before the watershed INF Treaty was concluded, but not without force and pertinence:

> In no other organized endeavor of the nations of mankind has so much work been expended to so little effect as in the efforts to achieve arms control. We must suppose that there has been something fundamentally wrong at the conceptual level to account for so consistent a failure on so large a scale over so long a period.[49]

In the United States, formal arms control is undertaken as executive agreements or treaties. The Congress, through the Arms Control and Disarmament Act of 1961, has ensured that the President cannot independently pursue arms control. That act prohibits the President from taking action under any law to "obligate the United States to disarm or to reduce or to limit the . . . armaments of the United States except

---

[48]The works of Grant Hammond and Albert Wohlstetter cited in Chapter 1, supra, are pertinent in this regard.

[49]Louis J. Halle, *The Elements of International Strategy: A Primer for the Nuclear Age,* vol. 10 (Lanham, Md.: University Press of America, 1984), 73.

pursuant to the treaty making power of the President under the Constitution or unless authorized by further affirmative legislation by the Congress of the United States."[50]

In addition to the formal, positive constraints of arms control agreements, the United States has agreed to "negative security assurances." These arise in cases where the United States seeks arms control agreements from others, and assures them of its good intentions in order to secure their assent. With regard to the Non-Proliferation Treaty, for example, the United States has pledged not to "use nuclear weapons against any non-nuclear-weapon State party to the Non-Proliferation Treaty or any comparable internationally binding commitment not to acquire nuclear explosive devices, except in the case of an attack on the United States, its territories or armed forces, or its allies."[51]

This is not the place to detail all the constraints that arms control has placed on the use of force.[52] For the decision maker or the war fighter they have the overall effect of removing options from the board. For potential adversaries, they offer opportunities to their asymmetrical advantage. If, for example, there are no chemical weapons in the arsenal because they have been proscribed by prior agreement on arms control, then the option of retaliating against the use of chemical weapons in kind has been removed from the list of possible responses. Perhaps as important, they are not available to deter the use of chemicals. Other options, perforce, must be considered. Thus, when a prospective user of chemical weapons against a state that has none calculates the possible responses, it can rule out a response in kind, and try to determine the prospects of a stronger or a weaker response, and whether those prospects are tolerable. The credibility of a stronger deterrent response is thus brought under intense pressure, raising questions of necessity and proportionality to new heights.

The number and variety of constraints imposed on the use of military force by legal and arms control strictures are impressive. They affect

---

[50] 22 USC § 2573 (1964).

[51] *The Arms Control Reporter* (Brookline, Mass.: Institute for Defense and Disarmament Studies, 1991), 860-4.2.

[52] A compilation of arms control treaties can be found at <http://www.state.gov/www/global/arms/bureau_ac/treaties_ac.html>.

not only the conduct of armed conflict, but training, organizing, and equipping for it as well. For the most part they are additional to organizational and operational constraints, further increasing the overall burden on decision makers and war fighters. Moreover, it must be acknowledged that legal and arms control constraints affect only those who abide by them. To the extent that actors (states, groups, or individuals) proceed in disregard of legal and arms control norms, they are acting asymmetrically.

CHAPTER 4

Moral Constraints

America will not defend with its lives what it cannot defend with its conscience.

William Safire

It is both Christian and an act of love to kill the enemy without hesitation, to plunder and burn and injure him by any method until he is conquered, except that one must beware of sin and not to violate wives and virgins.

Martin Luther

Deeply rooted in the American psyche is a moral presumption against the use of force. It underlies the other sources of constraint—operational, organizational, and legal—but can be separated from them because it goes beyond them. Regardless of the other constraints, in order even to consider the use of force, Americans must find release from powerfully ingrained moral strictures. The sources of such moral constraints—whether they arise from basic Judeo-Christian teachings, from the Enlightenment, or from other sources—need not detain this analysis. It suffices here to note their existence and to seek to appreciate their depth and breadth.

In interpersonal disagreements as well as in matters of statecraft, the use of force or violence has long been viewed as the *ultima ratio*. Civilized persons and states were discouraged from resorting to force to resolve disagreements; such a resort was said to signal a moral failure to resolve contentious issues peacefully. This is, in part, why it has been important in U.S. policy to demonize adversaries. From the "savage" Indians of the Wild West to the Kaiser, Hitler, and Tojo, through the North Korean "gooks" to Ho Chi Minh, and on to Qadhafi, "Pineapple Head" Noriega, "Hitlerite" Saddam Hussein, and Osama bin Laden, the opponent had to be characterized as evil incarnate. This helped to ease those moral reservations that suppress the use of force. It also brought pressure on constraints, and, in addition, quelled inclinations toward negotiation, accommodation, or appeasement instead of fighting. Thus, "It is obviously difficult for the layman to perceive a moral role for negotiations in a war against unmitigated evil, while, in a war of lesser consequence, there will be strong pressure for a negotiated settlement on the grounds that almost any peace is preferable to war."[1]

Similar to operational constraints, but evaluated on a different plane, moral reservations against the use of force also stem from considerations of *ends*, *ways*, and *means*. Some ends, or goals, are deemed to be immoral, as are some ways, or strategies to attain those goals, as are some means, or instruments. Because analyses must be made at each level, inevitable conflicts and paradoxes arise.

Sometimes the disagreements are genuinely polar. The American realist argument that the use of force should always be in the furtherance of national interests—*ends*—for example, "tends to ignore the fact that the calculation of what constitutes the national interest is itself an exercise in moral judgment, not an exercise in algebra."[2] Yet, from a perspective altered only slightly, George Kennan argues that basic national interests evince no moral content:

> The interests of a national society for which a government has to concern itself are basically those of its military security, the integrity of its political life, and the well-being of its people. These needs have no moral quality. . . . They are the unavoidable necessities of a national existence and therefore not subject to classification as either 'good' or 'bad.'[3]

Perhaps reconciliation of the two positions requires acceptance of a genuine bifurcation: that some core national interests—the survival of the state and the well-being of its people—inhere in the nature of the state and are common to all states in the international system. Others, such as imperialism, the spread of an ideology, such as communism, military conquest, humanitarian intervention, and even democratic evan-

---

[1]Joseph McMillan, "Talking to the Enemy: Negotiations in Wartime," *Comparative Strategy* 11, 4 (October/December 1992): 459.

[2]George Weigel, "The Poverty of Conventional Realism," in Cromartie, *Might and Right*, 85.

[3]George Kennan, "Morality and Foreign Policy," *Foreign Affairs*, Winter 1985–1986, 206, quoted in Finn, "Morality and Foreign Policy," in Cromartie, *Might and Right*, 39.

gelism, have high moral content. If this is a fair description of the split, then one could argue that there exist fundamental interests, or ends, the protection and furtherance of which offers prima facie moral justification for the use of force. In addition, there are other ends that might be pursued, the moral justification for which must be determined. This, of course, leaves open the question of the appropriateness of ways and means to attain those ends, and whether they are of the first (prima facie) or second (open to determination) order.

The evaluation of the morality of ends is rendered more complex by considerations of perspective, or levels of analysis. All too frequently, international actions are judged uncritically under the same set of rules and with the same moral template that interpersonal situations are assessed. Yet, what actions a state may morally and legally undertake are fundamentally different from what individuals may morally and legally do. Dean Acheson articulated the difference over thirty years ago: "A good deal of trouble comes from the anthropomorphic urge to regard nations as individuals. . . . The fact is that nations are not individuals; the cause and effect of their actions are wholly different."[4] Indeed, as Joseph Nye points out, "A simple-minded transposition of individual moral maxims to relations *among* states can lead to immoral consequences. When there are such gaps between our moral institutions and the consequences of following them, it is easier to moralize than to act morally. The Oxford students who in 1933 vowed never to fight may well have encouraged Hitler in his belief that Britain would not resist his aggression."[5]

Sometimes the moral dilemma is expressed as a question of *ways*. The ends might be agreed, but the strategy to attain them might be at issue on moral grounds. According to Arnold Kanter and Linton Brooks, "Many Americans believe that a nation committed to the rule of law cannot legitimately impose its will on others absent a clear and compelling threat. For them it is intervention, not inaction, that threatens the American soul."[6] Even though some uses of military force might

---

[4]Dean Acheson, "Ethics in International Relations Today," *Amherst Alumni News* (Winter 1965): 2–3, quoted in Finn, "Morality and Foreign Policy," in Cromartie, *Might and Right*, 38. The classic work on this subject is Reinhold Neibuhr, *Moral Man and Immoral Society: A Study in Ethics and Politics* (New York: Scribner, 1960).

[5]Joseph S. Nye, Jr., "Ethics and Intervention," in Miller and Smith, *Ideas and Ideals*, 127. Emphasis in the original.

[6]Kanter and Brooks, *U.S. Intervention Policy*, 39.

meet the criterion for military necessity, they might nevertheless be considered immoral. A good example might be to force troops to march through a minefield in order to attain an operational objective.[7]

Economic embargoes and blockades as a way to achieve political goals have often been criticized because they tend to work their effects on the innocent—the impoverished, the children, and the elderly— rather than the targets of the measures—the politico-military leadership. Thus, according to one account, "More than 500,000 children have died in Iraq because of the international embargo enforced in 1990, Iraq said in a report to the UN human rights commission in Geneva this week. . . . Iraqi Health Minister Umid Medhat Mubarak . . . put the total death toll under the embargo at 1,294,882, saying 523,204 of them were children below the age of five."[8] Killing innocents, or killing without justification, has long been the central touchstone of immorality.

Often, paradoxically, the more efficient the means of conducting warfare, the more difficult they will be to rationalize with ends. Nuclear weapons offer the most straightforward example of this conflictual situation. While nuclear weapons are very efficient, some would argue that *any* nuclear weapon use would be disproportionate and therefore immoral. There is evidence that such thinking has taken place at the highest levels of the U.S. government—the National Command Authority: "In long private conversations with successive Presidents— Kennedy and Johnson—I recommended, without qualification, that they never initiate, under any circumstances, the use of nuclear weapons. I believe they accepted my recommendation."[9] Divorced as it was from any operational, organizational, or legal context, this advice offered by the then-Secretary of Defense was clearly morally and means-based.

Efficient means may be popular, but that does not address the question of whether they are moral or not. "Opinion polls [of the U.S. public] showed that, late in the war [World War II], even urban bombing was favored by a majority of Americans. The prevailing opinion was

---

[7]"When we come to a mine field our infantry attacks exactly as if it were not there." Marshal Zhukov, quoted in Dwight D. Eisenhower, *Crusade in Europe* (Garden City, N.Y.: Doubleday, 1948), 468.

[8]"500,000 Children Perish in Iraq," *Gulf Daily News* (Bahrain), April 14, 2000.

[9]Robert S. McNamara, "The Military Role of Nuclear Weapons: Perceptions and Misperceptions," *Foreign Affairs*, Fall 1983, 79.

that war is terrible but necessary, and the greatest kindness would be its swift and favorable outcome. This 'imperative of victory' perspective is the most sympathetic one from which to view strategic bombardment, but it is not a moral case. Moral judgments are based on consistent frameworks of principles and the degree to which practice conforms to these precepts. Popularity can never excuse moral laxity."[10]

Others would take the position that achieving the same results by an extended attrition over a long period of time is comparatively less moral than using the most efficient means because greater cumulative harm would result. In this regard, "[t]he higher the rank of the persons killed, the more likely they are to be carriers of the purpose that is the legitimate target of hostilities. . . . The conclusion that follows from this runs directly counter to the conventional wisdom that has grown up recently about war, namely that among its worst features is the assassination of individuals."[11]

Within the overall moral aversion to the use of force lie other factors. The Western concept of fair play—of giving the underdog a chance, of recognizing the legitimate concerns and appeals of the underprivileged or oppressed—works as a constraint to the use of force. Uncritically extended from domestic considerations, such egalitarianism also influences policy. Superiority is viewed as something to be eschewed rather than embraced. Taken to its logical extremes, this line of reasoning results in the notion that "Whatever the goals for which it is fought, and whatever the methods it employs, no war can be just that does not rest on a rough balance of forces between the belligerents. . . . Since matching strength against weakness is unnecessary, by definition, it is also wrong."[12] The logical stretch here is truly extraordinary: the ends ("goals") and the ways ("methods") are, in van Creveld's opinion, irrelevant. Centrally important in this view is a balance of means, and without such a balance the use of force is morally wrong.

The contrapuntal argument to the egalitarian extremist was provided by Churchill: "You have not only to convince the Soviet Government

[10]Leo Mackay, Jr., review of Conrad C. Crane, *Bombs, Cities, and Civilians: American Airpower Strategy in World War II* (Lawrence: University of Kansas Press, 1993), *United States Naval Institute Proceedings*, December 1993, 97.

[11]Seabury and Codevilla, *War*, 227.

[12]Martin van Creveld, *The Transformation of War* (New York: The Free Press, 1991), 190.

that . . . they are confronted by superior force—but that you are not restrained by any moral consideration if the case arose from using that force with complete material ruthlessness."[13] James Turner Johnson provides a shrewd observation in this regard: "For if war is always presumptively wrong, the moral frame for policy debate over the use of force is reduced to the arena of those very limited exceptional circumstances that may override this presumption."[14]

Some means are considered unworthy or unchivalrous. As noted in Chapter 3, the strictures on dum-dum bullets from the Hague Convention of 1899 still apply, and the proscriptions against poison continue in effect. Poisons have long been associated with treachery, but their particular status seems to derive from "an aversion bordering on the instinctive, partly because their use is connected with the origins of life."[15] Beyond special constraints such as these two, the strongest arguments have been brought against the use of nuclear weapons and other weapons of mass destruction. The most cogent voices against nuclear use rose originally from those who had a hand in developing the weapons: Leo Szilard, George Kistiakowski, and Hans Bethe, for example. Guilt must play a role in their renunciation of, and campaigns against, nuclear weapons, but their conviction that nuclear use would be immoral has genuine roots.

Another example of means that raise moral issues is that of the blinding laser. Those who oppose use of lasers in this manner argue that deliberate blinding is immoral because it causes unnecessary suffering. The U.S. Department of Defense has indicated that it will not pursue lasers that have the purpose of blinding the enemy.[16] Land mines have

---

[13]Quoted in Spencer Warren, "Churchill's Realism: Reflections on the Fulton Speech," *The National Interest* (Winter 1995–1996): 48. Cf. "There is no real security in being just as strong as a potential enemy; there is security only in being a little stronger. There is no possibility of action if one's strength is fully checked; there is a chance for a positive foreign policy only if there is a margin of force which can be freely used." Nicholas J. Spykman, *America's Strategy in World Politics: The United States and the Balance of Power* (1942; reprint, Hamden, Conn.: Archon, 1970), 21.

[14]Johnson, "Broken Tradition," 34.

[15]Osgood and Tucker, *Force, Order, and Justice*, 217, footnote 36.

[16]The prohibition on blinding lasers has been formalized as Protocol IV to the *Convention on Prohibitions or Restrictions on the Use of Certain Conventional Weapons Which May Be Deemed to Be Excessively Injurious or to Have Indiscriminate Effects*. The Protocol entered into force on July 30, 1998. " 'We [the United States] are not parties to it but we are abiding by it,' Parks [W. Hayes Parks, special assistant to the U.S. Army's Judge Advocate General] said." David Atkinson, "New Weapons Technologies Offer Complex Issues for Review," *Defense Daily*, September 1, 1999, 2.

met a similar fate, on the argument that they have their greatest effect not on the battlefield, but indiscriminately on innocents. In December 1997 the Land Mine Treaty, banning the use, production, stockpiling and transfer of antipersonnel land mines, was signed at Oslo, Norway. Citing the need for land mines in Korea, the United States did not sign the treaty, but left open the possibility of accession to the treaty in the future.

The upshot of this discussion of ends, ways, and means when it comes to moral judgments on the use of force is that, difficult as it is, all must be satisfactorily accommodated. As Joseph Nye cautions, "One of the most common pitfalls in moral reasoning is 'one-dimensional ethics' in which an action is justified because it has good motives or because it has good consequences. But in common practice, people tend to make ethical judgments along three dimensions: motives, means, and consequences; and this introduces additional complexity and degree into ethical judgments."[17] Thus, Nye introduces the notion of intentions or motives. Motives have not been analyzed here because it was assumed that the motive for the use of force would have to be acceptable—or at least maintain a veneer of clear acceptability. When the issue is constraining the use of force, the "additional complexity and degree" referred to by Nye means that only the combination of manifestly acceptable ends, ways, means, and motives will permit force to be employed. Reservations in any of them will probably eventuate in a constraint.

Some moral constraints are peculiar to a certain nationality. Here, one would note the deep reservation the United States would have on using nuclear weapons against an Asiatic people, almost regardless of the provocation. Clearly, fearing the racist label, U.S. decision makers would be morally constrained from nuclear use against Asians, and probably also against other nonwhite races. In his study of self-deterrence, John Lewis Gaddis wrote:

> The fact that the only prior use of the bomb had been against Asians now came back to haunt the Truman administration as reports from the United Nations and from embassies overseas stressed the extent to which the weapon had come to be seen as a racist instrument. The impression was developing, Saudi Arabia's United Nations delegate told Eleanor Roosevelt, that the bomb was intended for use against

---

[17]Nye, "Ethics and Intervention," in Miller and Smith, *Ideas and Ideals*, 132.

'colored people.' Indian Prime Minister Jawaharlal Nehru warned of the 'wide-spread feeling in Asia that the bomb was intended for use only against Asiatics.' "[18]

In efforts to demonstrate superior morality, U.S. policy makers often go beyond the letter of any law or other requirement to constrain possibilities on the use of force. Arms Control Impact Statements have been used for years in order to ensure U.S. compliance with arms control agreements. In some cases, however, they have gone far beyond compliance issues, causing hardware manufacturers to adhere to guidelines much more stringent than the letter of the law required. Thus, restrictions were applied to Patriot and Aegis systems so that they would remain well clear of the confines of the *Treaty Between the United States of America and the Union of Soviet Socialist Republics On the Limitation of Anti-Ballistic Missile Systems* (1972 ABM Treaty). The fix for *Patriot* to permit the system to engage even the primitive Iraqi Scud missiles was just short of miraculous. Another, earlier, example was that of a Navy lawyer ruling that defensive minefields could not be laid in the Philippine archipelagic waters because they would violate the spirit of the Washington and London Naval Treaties. Of late, in the United States, the development of an antisatellite weapon has been inhibited by arguments that it would not be proper to militarize space. Finally, there are concerns about the environment. Training and operations have been hampered, and in some cases prevented, by environmental or ecological concerns. The U.S. Navy's struggle with the citizens of the island of Vieques is but the latest chapter in this extended conflict. Given that untrained forces cannot perform as effectively as trained ones, this acts

---

[18]John Lewis Gaddis, "The Origins of Self-Deterrence: The United States and the Non-Use of Nuclear Weapons 1945–1958," in *The Long Peace: Inquires into the History of the Cold War*, John L. Gaddis (New York: Oxford University Press, 1987), 119. Cf. "When the besieged French in Dien Bien Phu were desperate, French and U.S. military leaders considered the possibility of relieving the fortress by using U.S. air strikes against the Vietnamese attackers. Within the U.S. military, discussion favored the use of low-yield nuclear weapons for that purpose. President Eisenhower later told his biographer that when these discussions were reported to him, he responded: 'You boys must be crazy. We can't use those awful things against Asians for a second time in less than ten years. My God.' Self-deterrence was as effective as mutual deterrence." Carl Kaysen, Robert S. McNamara, and George W. Rathjens, "Nuclear Weapons after the Cold War," *Foreign Affairs*, Fall 1991, 95–110.

as a constraint on the use of force: decision makers will be reluctant to send untrained troops to apply force in a given instance. In each of these examples, the forcing function had little or nothing to do with operational, organizational, or legal considerations.

Ultimately, the issues of the morality of ends, ways, and means become circular and are essentially irresolvable. Seabury and Codevilla put a nice point on it when they wrote, "Since war (insofar as it is not madness or mere tribal conflict) is the clash of different moral standards, we agree with Clausewitz that violent means are rightly the mere servants of political considerations. Nevertheless, we maintain that any attempt to resolve definitively the natural tension between the demands of military operations and those of political authority is fraught with danger."[19]

---

[19]Seabury and Codevilla, *War*, 12.

CHAPTER 5

Effects

Some of our favorite threats are beginning to lose all credibility with potential adversaries. We are not likely ever again to conduct an amphibious landing against a hostile beach (the last one occurred at Inchon, Korea, in 1950) or drop large numbers of paratroopers behind enemy lines (the last time was during World War II), as these are very risky enterprises. We are not likely to be torpedoing commercial ships because of danger to their crews and the potential for environmental damage from the spilled cargoes.

Harvey M. Sapolski

As a result of the Gulf War, this is now well understood. If offered war, the West will reply that the invitation can only be accepted on its terms. Public opinion must be supportive, the result pre-ordained, and the conflict structured as a contest between conventional forces. As an exchange of fire it must be confined to military units, and avoid spilling over into civil society. If targets that are both civil and military are attacked, the objective must be to disable rather than to hurt—to deny fighting forces their supplies, their energy and their leadership. With the possible exception of China on an issue it believes to be essential to its territorial integrity, it is hard for the moment to envisage conflicts in which an enemy will engage us on anything approaching these terms.

Lawrence Freedman

Unquestionably, the most important effect of the various constraints on the use of force is that they have direct and powerful impact on *centers of gravity*. In military parlance, the center of gravity is "Those characteristics, capabilities, or localities from which a military force derives its freedom of action, physical strength, or will to fight."[1] As a critical focus for military operations, there is no substitute for the center of gravity: it is the prime mover, the engine of military effectiveness. Military actions seek to attack the adversary's center of gravity, while at

---

[1] U.S. Department of Defense, *DOD Dictionary of Military and Associated Terms*. Joint Publication 1-02. <http://www.dtic.mil/doctrine/jel/doddict/> (Accessed May 5, 2000).

the same time assiduously providing sanctuary for one's own. Constraints on the use of force weigh heavily on the ability both to attack and neutralize an adversary's "freedom of action, physical strength, or will to fight," and on one's ability to use one's own center of gravity— freedom of action, physical strength, or will to fight—to best advantage. In this way, constraints have a double-edged effect.

If the thesis of this book is correct—that constraints on the use of the U.S. armed forces are increasing along four major axes, and that those constraints jeopardize U.S. security by their influence on both one's own and the adversary's centers of gravity—the effects should be observable. It would be satisfying, both intellectually and analytically, if a straight cause and effect line could be drawn between constraints and their outcomes. How powerful it would be to say that operational constraints lead directly to mission failure. Or to suggest that, in the main, organizational constraints affect whether or not force is used at all, and if it is, at what level of intensity. Such responses would offer insight and a giant step toward determining what remedial actions should be taken. Unfortunately, the subject is complex enough, and the constraints diverse enough, that straight-line causes and effects are not in evidence. One of the principal arguments of this effort, moreover, is that any particular constraint might be important, helpful, humane, desirable—or any combination of those. It is not the individual impact of constraints that is at issue, but their cumulative effect.

Thus, this chapter seeks to tally the overall effects of the constraints. It proposes that the effects manifest themselves in two important areas: *threats to use force*, which are key to deterrence, and *the employment of military force*, which is an issue of effectiveness. In the first instance, the greatest good is represented by the absence of the use of force while obtaining one's objectives. Given the fact that the West in general and the United States in particular have assumed a strategic posture that is defensive in nature, deterrence of conflict is to be greatly desired. Constraints on the use of force that undermine deterrence should be carefully scrutinized, for one must ask, "Can the use of force be credibly threatened if an adversary is convinced that U.S. self-imposed restrictions make its use unlikely?"[2] In the second instance,

---

[2]Jeffrey Record, *Perils of Reasoning by Historical Analogy: Munich, Vietnam, and American Use of Force since 1945*. Occasional Paper No. 4 (Maxwell Air Force Base, Ala.: Air University, March 1998), 24.

focusing on constraints on the actual employment of force, the approach should address how and why the effectiveness of the use of force is affected by the constraints. In this manner, this chapter assesses the aggregated effects of constraints on the use of force.

States maintain military forces and adopt policies to use them for many reasons. For those forces to have value, they must be capable of being used effectively. Obsolescent or obsolete forces have low credibility and low operational serviceability. Likewise, forces heavily bound in a variety of strictures—no matter how powerful and ready they appear—will, no doubt, find their projected influence deeply undermined.

Obviously, the United States intends to have it both ways. It wants to wield power and influence, and, at the same time, it desires to project a peaceful, benign image. As the lone superpower on the world scene, the United States presents a deeply conflicted image. It wants to "engage" other states and to "shape" events, while not donning the mantle of "global policeman." As the leading democracy, it seeks to set an example for nonviolent settlement of interstate quarrels. Yet, the United States attempts to pursue this path in a disorderly world, one that finds others not particularly inclined to follow the U.S. lead.

Attempting to have it both ways—establishing a very powerful, threatening posture while offering assurances of benign intentions—illuminates the fundamentally paradoxical nature of the problem. In order to deter effectively, one must credibly either threaten dire consequences or project a willingness to deny perpetrators their objectives. Once the use of force has been decided upon, in order to fight effectively and efficiently, one should pursue operational superiority so that conflict will be short and ensuing casualties and damage low. It is precisely in these critical areas—the credibility of deterrence and the effectiveness of the actual use of force—that constraints deliver their greatest damage.

Constraints and Deterrence

It is impossible to prove the negative. If something does not happen, who can say with confidence that the lack of action was the result of one's policy or in spite of it? What can be assessed, however, is the perceptions of those who brought about the use of force against them. That is, because one cannot determine with high confidence why something did not happen, one must learn from incidents that did. So, to study deterrence, one must rely on deterrence failures.[3]

Did not North Korea, with Soviet complicity, misinterpret U.S. willingness to fight for the security and independence of South Korea? Is it not clear that Castro and Khrushchev misunderstood U.S. resolve in 1962 in placing missiles in Cuba? Can anyone argue persuasively that Ho Chi Minh anticipated in the early 1960s that the United States would commit as many as half a million troops to the defense of South Vietnam? Did the Argentines believe the British would travel eight thousand miles in force to oust them from the Falklands in 1982? Could Qadhafi have guessed that the United States would conduct an aerial raid on Libya in response to a discotheque bombing in Germany? Could Noriega have expected that the United States would attack and capture him in Panama in January 1990? Is it not a fact that Saddam Hussein was convinced that he could annex Kuwait without large-scale interference from without, and that no coalition could be formed that could, in a ferocious, massive air and land attack, forcibly remove his army from that country? In each of these cases, the antagonist was militarily inferior to the forces arrayed against it. In each, also, the antagonist considered the risks of the action it was taking and opted to assume them. The reason, in large measure, is that the West in general, and the United States in particular, have projected either images of reluctance to use force to protect their interests, or the messages they conveyed were so ambiguous that the antagonists misinterpreted or incorrectly assessed them. Consequently, deterrence failed.

Logically, there is a third explanation: The threats to take action were powerful and unambiguous, but the perpetrator opted to ignore them regardless of the consequences. This explanation describes an irrational adversary who, knowing that he will be severely punished or that he cannot attain his objectives, transgresses anyway. On the other hand, it might describe a rational adversary whose primary intention is to inflict pain on a victim. It is likely that the attacks on Khobar Towers in 1996, the USS *Cole* in 2000, and the World Trade Center and Pentagon in 2001 fell into this latter category. No amount of credible capability or determined opposition can reliably deter such acts.

---

[3]To study deterrence directly would mean that one would have to interview a prospective aggressor and be informed of the reason he did not attack. It is likely that such prospects would neither submit to an interview, nor that they would be truthful.

Deterrence depends on capability and the will to use it. It takes two forms. First, there is "general" deterrence, which is relied upon broadly to keep the peace. General deterrence stems from amassing the capability and projecting the will to inflict severe damage in retaliation on those who would disturb the peace. Merely by maintaining a large, highly capable, ready military, the United States conveys its ability to punish those who would transgress against it. By assuming a similar posture, any state can exercise general deterrence.

As well as through punishment, general deterrence can work through denial. Under deterrence by denial, those who would harm the United States, or its interests, are, as a matter of deliberate policy, not permitted to attain their objectives. Recognizing that they cannot succeed, they are deterred from making the attempt. To achieve deterrence by denial, first one attempts to make hostile acts as difficult as possible to carry out, and then, should such an act take place, to thwart attainment of its goals. This is the approach used against those on whom punishment would be ineffective or infeasible—terrorists, hostage takers, and extortionists, for example. The message is: You cannot prevail, so why make the attempt?

General deterrence through the threat of punishment requires maintaining the capability and credibly projecting the will to use it. General deterrence through denial requires maintaining stout defenses to thwart easy faits accomplis and a history of staunch refusals to yield to coercive threats.

In contrast to general deterrence, "focused" or "immediate" deterrence—the second form of deterrence—operates at a different level of specificity. It recognizes that, sometimes, general deterrence won't work—merely collecting and parading a military arsenal will be viewed as weak, irresolute, or irrelevant—and that a focused, immediate, or specific deterrent threat or statement will be required. General deterrence failed in the case of the British and the Argentines over the Falkland Islands in 1982. It failed again in the Persian Gulf in 1990. In both of those cases, the aggressor transgressed against the interests of a nuclear-armed state, concluding no doubt that a general deterrent was insufficient. Either powerful active and passive military forces (capability), or a specific deterrent statement (will), or perhaps both, was needed to forestall aggression. None of these occurred.

Thus, compared to general deterrence, focused deterrence is the more powerful form of deterrence. It is greatly hamstrung by political considerations, however. Policy makers rarely exhibit a willingness to issue a concrete deterrent threat, opting instead for more flexible, diffuse approaches that permit greater maneuvering room.

Both general and immediate deterrence can operate through threat of punishment or by denial. Deterrence by threat of punishment requires identifiable targets and works best on organized groups that can be located and attacked—governments, for example. For individuals or for organizations that are less formal and more difficult to locate—terrorists, or computer hackers, for example—deterrence by denial is the more appropriate form.

Deterrence by punishment and denial both require capability and will. Since the end of the Cold War, the United States has enjoyed military superiority over all countries of the world. So, for deterrence through the threat of punishment, the capability factor in the equation has remained virtually overwhelming. The United States maintains the capability to use force up to and including the nuclear devastation of any country or locatable organization in the world. Sheer capability to punish, therefore, is not at issue. With respect to deterrence by denial, however, defenses tend to be inadequate. On the capability side of the deterrence equation, therefore, deterrence by threat of punishment is strong, but deterrence by denial is open to challenge.

Will extends across both general and immediate deterrence, and it applies whether deterrence is by threat of punishment or through denial. For deterrence by threat of punishment, the willingness for general deterrence appears strong, while will for immediate deterrence is problematical. It depends on the United States recognizing a particular threat and then issuing a deterrent statement specifically addressing it. On the other hand, for deterrence by denial, the U.S. history with respect to dealing with terrorism or extortion is essentially unblemished.

Will is communicated in a number of ways. Sometimes it is part of a declaratory policy. Sometimes it is conveyed by demonstration—by the use of the capability, either in actual operations or in exercises. If neither of these takes place, then deterrence is general.

The ability to convey will is very complex. Its framework extends across actions and geography both in the present and in the future. When Ronald Reagan was elected President in 1980, one of the first actions of his new administration was to fire the striking air traffic controllers. After an extended period of negotiations, the head of the air controllers' union made a public statement to the effect that the union had failed to appreciate the new President's resolve, and that Ronald Reagan was one tough negotiator. Following the presidency of Jimmy Carter, can there be any doubt that this statement was read with great sobriety in the Kremlin? The point is that deterrence pivots on will, and will is constructed and maintained by the whole panoply of actions by the leadership. The coupling between domestic and foreign policy is close in a democracy. The effect of actions taken in one realm must always be evaluated from the point of view of the other.

Adversaries constantly assess and reassess the deterrent projection of capability and will. If they perceive will to be weak, they will not be deterred.[4] Ralph Peters opines that "We will face opponents for whom treachery is routine, and they will not be impressed by tepid shows of force with restrictive rules of engagement."[5] But the issue is not necessarily bound up in treachery; it is more a matter of cold calculation.

Adversaries watch and learn. They assiduously study their prospective enemies, searching for and cataloging weaknesses. Adversaries "[r]espect the U.S. military establishment for its formidable strengths. They are also shrewd enough to circumvent those strengths and to exploit the vulnerabilities inherent in the rigid U.S. adherence to professional conventions regarding the use of force. As long as U.S. military policies are held hostage to such conventions, those vulnerabilities will persist."[6] Evidence exists, moreover, that the perception of some adversaries, at least, is that U.S. *will* is in short supply; viz.: "Mr. [Charles] Freeman, former deputy chief of mission in the U.S. Embassy in Beijing, said Chinese officials told him Washington would not defend Taiwan in a dispute with China because American leaders lack resolve."[7] Examples of foreign perceptions

---

[4]According to Patrick Glynn, "In the twentieth century, those powers least prone to choose war as a vehicle of policy have also been *a fortiori* the least prone to take the steps necessary to prevent other powers from choosing it." "The Sarajevo Fallacy—The Historical and Intellectual Origins of Arms Control Theology," *The National Interest* 9 (Fall 1998): 30.

[5]Ralph Peters, "The New Warrior Class," *Parameters* 24, 2 (Summer 1994): 24.

[6]Andrew J. Bacevich, "The Limits of Orthodoxy: The Use of Force after the Cold War," in Aspen, *United States Use of Force*, 185.

[7]Bill Gertz, "General Who Threatened L.A. Tours U.S. on Chinese Mission," *Washington Times*, December 18, 1996, 6.

of one's will, such as this one, tend to be rare. It is difficult to take them at face value, but one is obliged not to ignore them either.

Figure 1 summarizes the discussion on capability and will for general and focused deterrence through punishment and denial and assesses U.S. effectiveness:

		GENERAL DETERRENCE	FOCUSED DETERRENCE
CAPABILITY	PUNISH	STRONG	STRONG
	DENY	DEFENSES INADEQUATE	DEFENSES SUSPECT
WILL	PUNISH	QUESTIONABLE	UNADDRESSED
	DENY	STRONG	UNADDRESSED

Figure 1[8]

Figure 1 provides the following insights: General deterrence has some strong points, but also some weaknesses both in capability and in will. Focused deterrence leaves much to be desired, especially in the projection of will. The capability to punish is uniformly powerful, but the will to punish is either questionable or weak. The capability and will to deny suffer from some important shortcomings. All in all, general deterrence seems to be clearly stronger than focused deterrence, while capability in both deterrence areas is, for the most part, comparably stronger than will.

Considering deterrence in this frame of reference, when one contemplates actions with regard to certain types of weapons, therefore, broad questions of deterrence and overall strategy and policy, rather than narrow conceptions of military utility, should prevail. Nevertheless, in

---

[8]The figure, and much of the discussion of deterrence, was contained in Roger W. Barnett, "Information Operations, Deterrence, and the Use of Force," *Naval War College Review* 51, 2 (Spring 1998): 7–19.

the recent past, issues regarding antisatellite weapons and ballistic missile defenses, to suggest only two examples, have been decided on the latter rather than the former. As Colin Gray points out, "The same intellectual and historical error which claims that weapons make war, naturally encourages the fallacy that the absence of weapons—or perhaps of bad, destabilizing weapons—makes peace. . . . The great issues of war and peace are reduced, on this logic, to the technological and administrative details of force postures and military procedures."[9] As for the notion that certain weapons should not be acquired lest they stimulate the very conflict they were intended to deter, Gray continues: "The idea that the intended means of deterring war might themselves inadvertently trip the war that they were designed to deter, is an interesting and (in principle) important one. However, while being ever alert to this possibility, it is difficult to find historical evidence in its support."[10]

Security for those "civilized" states today continues to depend on their own exertions to establish capability and will, but it also depends in increasing measure on the restraint of their enemies. The vulnerability of all states of the world to intercontinental nuclear missile attack is legendary. The very existence of each and every state depends on restraint—for whatever reason—on the part of the owners of intercontinental range nuclear-tipped missiles. This condition of total national vulnerability came about only with the marriage of nuclear weapons with such long-range delivery vehicles. Reminders of that vulnerability to influence policy appear from time to time, as during the China-Taiwan crisis in the spring of 1996: " 'Some Chinese lower-level officials told some visiting American officials that we wouldn't dare defend Taiwan because they'd rain nuclear bombs on Los Angeles,' said Winston Lord, assistant secretary of state for East Asia and the Pacific."[11] The qualitative power of this threat cannot be overemphasized. The very existence of states now hinges on the forbearance of those who possess large arsenals of long-range nuclear arms.

---

[9]Colin S. Gray, "The Definitions and Assumptions of Deterrence: Questions of Theory and Practice," *The Journal of Strategic Studies* 13, 4 (December 1990): 12.

[10]Ibid.

[11]"Nuclear Warning to US Cited," *Boston Globe,* March 18, 1996, 4. The strategic wisdom of such a threat is highly questionable, however. It would seem that the People's Republic of China would, above all, avoid actions that would provoke a nuclear fight with a United States vastly superior in nuclear weaponry.

To be sure, adversaries do not want to be deterred. From the incidence of terrorism, skyjacking, and hostage taking, it seems evident that the greater the disparity of military power between adversaries, the greater the inclination of the weaker to resort to irregular or illegal—asymmetrical—warfare. The attractiveness of chemical, biological, and radiological weapons stems from similar considerations. International agreements and moral arguments will be to no avail against the selection of such asymmetrical means. Witness the following assertion attributed to the President of Iran: "Biological weapons are a poor man's atomic [bomb] and can be easily produced. We should at least consider them for our defense. . . . Although the use of such weapons is inhumane, the [Iran-Iraq] war taught us that international laws are only drops of ink on paper."[12] This, of course, notwithstanding the fact that Iran is a party to the Biological Weapons Treaty.[13] Radiological weapons have also been in the news, and the context is familiar:

> Washington fears that the Saudi terrorist Osama bin Laden is trying to develop an 'Islamic bomb.' . . . Customs officers from Uzbekistan discovered 10 lead-lined containers at a remote border crossing with Kazakhstan at the end of last month. These were filled with enough radioactive material to make dozens of crude weapons, each capable of contaminating a large area for many years. . . . Military analysts have described such 'radiation bombs' as 'poor man's nuclear weapons', in which conventional explosives are used to spread radioactive material. . . . Five years ago, Chechen rebels announced that they had planted a radiation bomb in a Moscow park. It was dug up by Russian bomb-disposal experts. Although it would have caused little damage

---

[12]Quoted in W. Seth Carus, *The Poor Man's Atomic Bomb? Biological Weapons in the Middle East*, Policy Papers Number 23 (Washington, D.C.: The Washington Institute for Near East Policy, 1991), 35. Or, more modestly, "Thus there are few apparent moral or religious impediments should Iran choose to employ NBC weapons against the United States. Assessments which fail to recognize that the Iranian justification for war has a significantly lower threshold than that established by Western just war doctrine could be dangerously misleading." Paula DeSutter, "Deterring Iranian NBC Use," *Strategic Forum no. 110* (Washington, D.C.: National Defense University, April 1997), <http://198.80.36.91/ndu/inss/strforum/forum110.html>.

[13]Formally, the Convention on the Prohibition of the Development, Production, and Stockpiling of Bacteriological (Biological) and Toxin Weapons and on their Destruction, 1972.

because it was buried, American experts say that such a bomb exploded above ground would be devastating.[14]

This attitude has, in fact, been encouraged by the inaction of states whose intentions did not match their actions. "Time and again treaties have proven illusory," Fred Ikle writes, "because the nations that relied on them lacked the will, or the means, to respond forcefully to violations."[15] The importance of the convergence of these factors cannot be downplayed.[16] As the example of Osama bin Laden's interest in radiological weapons indicates, this is no longer an issue for societies; the capability and the power are devolving.

The attempt on the part of the perpetrators is to negate the strength of the prospective deterrer, either by rendering his capability moot or irrelevant, or by sapping his will. Thus, adversaries will take asymmetrical actions that Westerners would consider immoral or reprehensible in order to negate the other's advantages. Indeed, forms of warfare have been practiced that seem unimaginable to the Western mind, and therefore supremely difficult to defend against. It has been pointed out, for example, that bacteriological warfare offers the prospects of selective targeting, which "could be achieved through the use of insect or animal vectors, and disease organisms biologically engineered to strike selectively according to age, gender, race, or behavior."[17] At a time when more than eight hundred American scientists have made a commitment not to conduct research on biological weapons[18]—which is not prohibited by the Biological Weapons Convention of 1972—this should be a matter of serious concern. The concern stems not from a desire to

---

[14]Julian West, "Atomic Haul Raises Fears of Bin Laden Terror Bomb," *London Sunday Telegraph*, April 23, 2000. This was nearly a year and a half before the attacks on the World Trade Center and the Pentagon.

[15]Fred C. Ikle, "The Next Lenin: On the Cusp of Truly Revolutionary Warfare," *The National Interest* (Spring 1997): 18.

[16]Frederick Timmerman warns, in the strongest of terms, "The society that acts resolutely to merge technology and psychology, all moral questions aside, will gain the decisive edge." "Future Warriors," *Military Review* (September 1987): 50–51.

[17]John F. Guilmartin, Jr., "Technology and Strategy: What Are the Limits?" in Howard and Guilmartin, *Two Historians*, 33.

[18]Larry Thompson, "The Perils of Biological Warfare," *Washington Post* (Health), January 24, 1989, 7.

develop biological weapons, but because if no research is conducted, one cannot anticipate future developments in the field, understand their potential effects, or prepare adequate countermeasures. Consider the confusion and uncertainty that surrounded the distribution of anthrax through the U.S. mail system following the September 2001 attacks. The concern is particularly acute because biological weapons "would be easier to make than chemical weapons and easier to acquire than nuclear material."[19] In a similar vein, reportedly Russia has developed an anthrax toxin that is antibiotic-resistant, along with three new nerve gas agents that "could be made without using any of the precursor chemicals . . . under the 1993 Chemical Weapons Convention."[20]

Credibility, both with one's own decision makers and with those of adversaries and prospective adversaries, is vital to military forces. That they can perform their assigned missions "faithfully and well" cannot be taken for granted, but must be indicated in some way. Actual military operations, opportunities to demonstrate high capability, tend to be few and far between. The majority of the weapon systems employed by the coalition forces in the Gulf War, for example, were unproven in actual conflict. Very often, moreover, modern weapon systems never find employment in actual combat. The United States has no contemporary naval personnel that have ever participated in actual antisubmarine warfare operations. It can count on one hand the members of all services who have participated in actual surface-to-surface or surface-to-air missilery as well. Before the Gulf War, the same was true for large-scale armored warfare and air-to-ground missile shooting. The point is that indications of military capability cannot rely on actual combat operations. They must be demonstrated in other ways—shows of force, exper-

---

[19]Ibid. Cf. "The disease was eradicated two decades ago, but the smallpox virus lives on, stored in freezers at a pair of research facilities in the United States and Russia. And, very likely, it remains alive in the possession of rogue nations. . . . Recent intelligence estimates suggest that countries that possess the virus or are seeking to acquire it include China, India, Pakistan, North Korea, Iraq, Iran, Israel, Cuba, and Yugoslavia." Steve Goldstein, "Old Scourge Kindles Fear of Biological Terrorism," *Philadelphia Inquirer*, April 2, 2000, 1.

[20]"Russia Reportedly Has New Poison," *Washington Post*, April 4, 1997, 17. At a Department of Defense news briefing on April 28, 1997, Secretary of Defense William Cohen said, "There are some reports . . . that some countries have been trying to construct something like an Ebola Virus, and that would be a very dangerous phenomenon, to say the least." Office of the Assistant Secretary of Defense (Public Affairs), *DoD News Briefing*, April 28, 1997. <http://www.://www.dtic.dla.mil:80/defenselink/news/Apr97/t042897_t0428coh.html> (Accessed May 13, 1997).

iments, and exercises, for example. To the extent that confusion reigns about the ability or the latitude to use force, both friends and adversaries wind up perplexed.

The threat, embedded in mutual assured destruction, of killing many civilians in retaliation for a strategic attack cannot help but have a corrosive effect over time. It leads to muddy thinking with respect to the deterrent relationship and about what constitutes success. To recall the assertion of John Pike, that the threat of retaliation would be sufficient to deter an attack with nuclear weapons ("The threat of retaliation deterred Joseph Stalin and Mao. Everybody recognizes that if you launch a nuclear attack on the United States, we would turn that country into a sea of radioactive glass in 30 minutes."[21]), in the first place, we can never know what deterred Stalin or Mao. We can not even determine with any degree of confidence that they were deterred. All we know is that they did not directly challenge the U.S. nuclear deterrent. On the other hand, evidence abounds that future adversaries might not be so respectful of a powerful retaliatory capability.[22]

Secondly, this qualifies as a classic description of a Pyrrhic Victory: We turn Ukraine into a sea of radioactive glass at the cost of ten? fifty? seventy-five? million dead Americans. Others understand the point in full measure. Well after the Gulf War had concluded, General Wafiaq Samarrai, former head of Iraqi military intelligence was quoted as saying, "Tell the allies that they have to destroy Iraq's biological agents before Saddam can use them. Iraq could attack its neighbors by missile, or America through terrorism. The United States might retaliate with nuclear weapons, but by then the disaster will already have happened."[23] This asymmetrical situation is truly terrifying, for if deterrence of a WMD attack fails and millions are killed in an initial strike, the question must be posed: What purpose would retaliation serve?

---

[21]Rowan Scarborough, "Missile Attack on U.S. Called Very Unlikely," *Washington Times*, December 12, 1991, A10.

[22]Robert Walpole, a National Intelligence Council official, reported to the Senate Governmental Affairs Subcommittee on Proliferation that "The probability that a missile with a weapon of mass-destruction would be used against U.S. forces or interests is higher today than during most of the Cold War, and will continue to grow." Quoted in "Gore's Secret Pact," *Wall Street Journal*, October 18, 2000, 26.

[23]Laurie Mylroie, "The World Trade Center Bomb: Who Is Ramzi Yousef? And Why It Matters," *The National Interest* (Winter 1995–1996): 14–15.

This is a very important point to grasp. If deterrence fails, the consequences are so severe that retaliation might serve no purpose whatsoever. The point is lost on those who have not thought the problem through. For example, the head of the Johns Hopkins University's Center for Civilian Biodefense said that "nothing the world has experienced in the last 100 years approaches the potential catastrophe of smallpox. The 1918 influenza pandemic, which killed an estimated 20 million worldwide, 'pales in comparison,' he said. More than 300 million people were killed by smallpox in the 20th century."[24] And yet, despite these horrifying numbers, "Henderson believes that the risk of smallpox being used by rogue states is small because it would invite massive retaliation."[25] This exemplifies the corrosive thought process spawned by the doctrine of mutual assured destruction (MAD). The central flaw in the theory of MAD was its central premise that deterrence could not fail. If deterrence failed, the results would be so catastrophic, so difficult even to theorize about, that deterrence must not fail. That was the mantra of those who advocated MAD: "You see, because of the threat of mutual destruction, deterrence cannot fail."

Those who championed mutual assured destruction against the Soviet Union could logically argue that large, survivable strategic forces offered a powerful deterrent to a massive nuclear attack. But they could never respond with an iota of persuasiveness about the ability of a MAD posture to deter, much less deal with, a small coercive nuclear, or a very devastating terrorist, attack. For this threat, MAD has no adequate answer except to say that the unknowns are so large that the Soviet Union would never dare to carry out such a threat. It has no answer whatsoever for terrorism.

The post-Cold War situation is vastly different. The concern about attacks from weapons of mass destruction—mainly nuclear or biological—arises from the possibility of deterrence failing for whatever reason, but the consequences of the failure of deterrence are unacceptable. If some "rogue" were able to deliver one nuclear weapon on, say, Seattle, killing hundreds of thousands, what would constitute an adequate response? Should the United States in response kill hundreds of thousands of the citizens of the

---

[24]Steve Goldstein, "Old Scourge Kindles Fear of Biological Terrorism," *Philadelphia Inquirer*, April 2, 2000, 1.

[25]Ibid.

rogue state in reprisal? What if the rogue had weapons in a secure reserve that could be used after the United States had retaliated, resulting in many more deaths in the United States? Other than to act as a stern exhortation to others who might have an interest in undertaking such an attack, what would retaliation accomplish? The fact of the failure of deterrence would mean that the United States would have lost whatever objectives it might have had—the price would have been too high. This is important enough to restate: as in the case of the hypothetical extortionate threat discussed in the introduction, *if deterrence of an attack with weapons of mass destruction fails, the matter is concluded: you lose.* There can be no adequate response, for it will either be grossly immoral to undertake, it will ignite even greater devastation, or both.

Fortunately, the barriers to nuclear, biological, or radiological weapon use are high. Those high barriers create a strangely convoluted situation, in which WMD do not adequately deter actions by rogue states, but their WMD would have high deterrent effect on first-world possessors of WMD. The difference, once again, has to do with perceptions of credibility and will. New acquirers of WMD have no track record of nonuse, no requirement not to set precedents, undoubtedly fewer constraints on their actions, and generally less to lose. They can project very powerful coercive threats—ones that the five nuclear-weapon-owning U.N. Security Council members, for example, clearly could not. The confluence of constraints on the use of force has created this perplexing and dangerous reversal of power. The issue being demonstrated is that WMD are not the problem; it is who owns them that matters.

One need not embrace Paul Ramsey's thesis, cited earlier, that "Whatever is wrong to do is wrong also to threaten"[26] in order to appreciate that great collateral damage would ensue from any large-scale nuclear exchange. To disbelieve that would be self-deception, pure and simple. In this regard, George Quester notes, "We similarly lied to ourselves when the Germans were starved into surrender in 1918, and when the Japanese were starved and bombed into surrender in 1945. . . . Obfuscations have let us live with deterrence."[27]

---

[26]Ramsey, "Political Ethics," in Kaplan, *Strategic Thinking*, 134–135.

[27]George H. Quester, "The Necessary Moral Hypocrisy of the Slide into Mutual Assured Destruction," in *Nuclear Deterrence and Moral Restraint: Critical Choices for American Strategy*, ed. Henry Shue (Cambridge: Cambridge University Press, 1989), 268.

Confusion exists in large measure because the various individual threads of U.S. national policy are not woven into a fabric, but are treated and acted on separately. The system is deconstructed and approached piecemeal rather than holistically. Thus, arms control and other international agreements constraining the use of force are reached without concern for the underlying strategic cloth. The Chemical Warfare Convention constitutes a case in point:

> The Clinton administration calls the chemical weapons treaty "the most ambitious arms control regime ever negotiated." Its ambition is matched only by that of the Kellogg-Briand Pact, also an American brainchild, also promulgated to great international applause. . . . All parties to that piece of paper pledged the renunciation of war forever. The year was 1928. Germany and Japan were signatories.[28]

In its rush to grasp this arms control nettle, the U.S. administration did not look insightfully at the deterrent fabric. Without chemical weapons (CW) for retaliation, how can the use of chemical weapons on U.S. forces be deterred? What retaliatory threat would ensure that potential CW users would hesitate—would reconsider? Of course, if nobody has CW, then deterrence is moot. But relinquishing a deterrent force in kind serves, ironically, to encourage proliferation by potential adversaries—who may well find that CW is the only advantage they might wield over the United States. If they believe nuclear retaliation for chemical use to be incredible, and consequently do not fear it, and if retaliation in kind has been deliberately relinquished, then chemical weapons for them appear extremely attractive as the weapon of choice.

The Chemical Weapons Convention (CWC) reveals yet another flawed U.S. conception of deterrence. In fact, there is manifest pessimism about deterrence of chemical weapon use, confirmed by the sheer amounts of defensive chemical warfare equipment and antidotes available in Army and Marine Corps ground units. They expect adversaries to use chemical weapons against them.[29] U.S. military leaders are

---

[28]Charles Krauthammer, "Peace through Paper . . . ," *Washington Post*, September 12, 1996, 27.

[29]Or else why would the United States have doubled its expenditures on chemical and biological defense programs, to the point where they now cost about $1 billion annually? U.S. Department of Defense, *Annual Defense Report, 2000,* 50. See also Linda D. Kozaryn, "Knowledge Key to Combating Chemical, Biological Warfare," American Forces Press Service, February 23, 1999.

resigned to being the recipient of first use of chemicals by the adversary. The United States has placed its CW deterrent on the back of accurate conventional weapons. But one cannot deter chemical use by threatening to do to the adversary that which might well be done to him in any event. An insufficient threat fails to force the enemy to pause, fails to force reconsideration of chemical use. The chary approach in the U.S. Senate to ratifying the CWC revealed an underlying suspicion about its viability. Perhaps senators recalled that "[I]n 1925, the U.S. Senate refused to ratify the Geneva Gas Protocol, probably helping to prevent German chemical victory in World War II. . . . The military advantages and allure of surreptitious chemical weapons virtually guarantee that the new treaty will be violated."[30] Worthy of note, in many of the states of concern, the production of CW need not even be surreptitious.

The case against biological weapons is that they are indiscriminate and cannot be controlled. That argues strongly for banning them, and, indeed, they have been prohibited by international agreement.[31] The case against chemical weapons, however, is qualitatively different, because they are not nearly so indiscriminate and can be rather carefully controlled. Banning chemical weapons by the CWC was more a case of "this is something that is ripe for doing, so let's do it," rather than for any other single reason. Such a ban is likely, among other things, to be fragile because of the ease of manufacture and the special horror of its use. In addition, because collateral damage is low, chemicals can be used domestically to control unruly groups.

Arguably, as yet another irony, chemicals can be more humane than conventional warfare. "Only 2% of U.S. chemical casualties in World War I died, as opposed to 25% of conventional casualties. Chemical weapons inflict clean kills with the vast majority of survivors able to expect full recovery—compared to the dismemberment, disfigurement, and permanent disabilities that occur from projectile weapons."[32] Consider the situation in Vietnam, at My Lai, if Lieutenant Calley had had

---

[30]Sherman McCall, "A Higher Form of Killing," *United States Naval Institute Proceedings* (February 1995): 44.

[31]The Bacteriological Weapons convention of 1972 has, at the time of this writing, 137 parties. U.S. Arms Control and Disarmament Agency, *Parties and Signatories of the Biological Weapons Convention*, November 4, 1996, Electronic Document, <http://www.acda.gov/treaties/bwcsig.txt> (Accessed March 31, 1997).

[32]McCall, "Higher Form," 43.

reliable control agents sufficient to temporarily disable the people who confronted him: massacre, crimes, and disgrace averted.

Representative of the arms control paradox—one can attain arms control agreements only when they are unnecessary[33]—the CWC demonstrates the triumph of hope over experience. The United States *hopes* that its adversaries will conform, for verification is impossible and sanctions for violations cannot be considered better than remote; they, in turn, recognize that this is one of the few sources of leverage they have. Chemical weapon employment against U.S. troops is only a matter of time. Thus does reliance on hope rather than strength turn policy into ashes.

Curiously, the United States, on the one hand, relies on technology to produce battlespace success, while on the other hand, its policy and organization seek stalemate. "This kind of victory-less war, first in Korea, then in Viet Nam and now in NATO war plans, suggests that the battle is thought of as being with the technology of the opponent, as if defeating a war machine defeats as well the process that set it in motion."[34] Yet, deterrence—general or focused, through punishment or denial—has been seen to hinge on capability and will. Restraints on the use of force debilitate deterrence by working against both.

The Environment: Tilting the Battlespace

Not only will deterrence be affected by the combination of capability and will—along with adversarial restraint—but operational results can suffer as well. Thus, "The United States can and undoubtedly will . . . fill its quiver with technologically superior arrows, but if it does not have the will to employ those arrows quickly and decisively, it may find itself less effective in conflict than its opponents."[35]

The United States wants to play by the rules, but the world environment has changed, and the old rules, the comfortable rules, often don't apply. The words of Adda Bozeman on this subject are instructive:

---

[33]This is a central theme of Colin S. Gray, *House of Cards: Why Arms Control Must Fail* (Ithaca, N.Y.: Cornell University Press, 1992).

[34]Robert Bathurst, "Two Languages of War," in *Soviet Military Thinking*, ed. Derek Leebart (London: George Allen & Unwin, 1981), 32.

[35]Richard Szafranski, "Peer Competitors, the RMA, and New Concepts: Some Questions," *Naval War College Review* 49, 2 (Spring 1996): 116.

Today, however, it is hardly ever possible to set interstate wars apart
from internal wars, revolutions, insurgencies, counterinsurgencies,
and the vast conglomerate of different species of guerrilla warfare or
irregular warfare. . . . [Such conflicts cannot] be analyzed or controlled by reference to standing rules of international law of war, for
these are addressed only to sovereign states.[36]

Bozeman continues, "A strong emotion prevails in the nation to
save our concept of peace from being swallowed by uncongenial concepts of war, an eventuality that would threaten the integrity of international law, which is anchored in the distinction between peace and
war."[37] Thus are legal constraints on the use of force applied to situations in which they are wholly unsuited.

Of course, the entire concept of what constitutes "war" has lost the
identity the law of armed conflict accords to it. Wars are typically no
longer declared, and they are no longer exclusively, or even ordinarily,
carried out by sovereign entities. In response to the life sentence
imposed on Sheik Omar Abdel Rahman for the 1993 bombing of the
World Trade Center, a powerful group of Muslim militants announced:
"The Americans have chosen war with Islam. . . . The Gamaa al-
Islamiya announces its vow to God that it will respond blow for blow.
American interests and people will be legitimate targets."[38] The Islamic
group clearly chose language that sought to justify its future acts in legal
terms, but in Western law the American people, as noncombatants, are
never legitimate targets.

Legal distinctions about warfare require the ability to distinguish
between combatants and noncombatants, and between aggressor and
defender. Except for World War II, "most conventional wars over the

---

[36]Adda B. Bozeman, "U.S. Conceptions of Democracy and Security in a World Environment of
Culturally Alien Political Thought: Linkages and Contradictions," in Sarkesian and Flanagan,
Domestic and National Agendas, 57–58.

[37]Ibid., 58.

[38]Douglas Jehl, "Islamic Group Vows Revenge on Americans," *New York Times*, January 22, 1996,
B-1. Cf. "Unnoticed by most Westerners, war has been unilaterally declared on Europe and the
United States. Fundamentalists are responding to what they see as a centuries-long conspiracy by
the West to destroy Islam." Daniel Pipes, "There Are No Moderates: Dealing with Fundamentalist
Islam," *The National Interest* (Fall 1995): 51.

last three centuries have been directed against soldiers."[39] But, in the future, an asymmetrical approach to conflict by antagonists will result in strategies that "will focus on obliterating the existing line between those who fight and those who watch, pay, and suffer."[40] In this regard, the Chinese book *Unrestricted War* offers some food for thought: "Unrestricted war is a war that surpasses all boundaries and restrictions. . . . It is the war of the future," its authors write. And, clearly to the point: " 'We are a weak country,' Wang [Xiangsui] said, 'so do we need to fight according to your rules? No.' "[41]

Strong measures that confine the use of force, that insist on clear delineation of peace and war, combatant and noncombatant, will result in great difficulty dealing with such strategies. Moreover, the trend has been to obscure the difference between the aggressor and the defender and the legal quality of a response to aggression.[42]

"Just war," the necessity to conduct warfare only when it serves a Western notion of justice, also works asymmetrically. Thus, "the concept of just war implies some minimum agreement concerning the larger moral order. It implies a symmetry on the part of the contending states. And it even implies some external authority to give some substance to the ground rules."[43] Note that none of these "implications" is true. No belligerent would contend that his effort is anything but just—and the adversary's is unjust, by definition. In the Soviet Union's classification of wars, for example, if a particular war served the purposes of socialism, it was labeled "just." In this frame of reference, socialist states were inca-

---

[39]Van Creveld, *Transformation of War*, 202.

[40]Ibid.

[41]John Pomfret, "China Ponders New Rules of Unrestricted War," *Washington Post*, August 8, 1999, 1. Wang Xiangsui was one of the authors of *Unrestricted War*. Osama bin Laden has been quoted thus: "We believe that the biggest thieves in the world are Americans and the biggest terrorists on earth are the Americans. The only way for us to defend against these assaults is by using similar means. We do not differentiate between those dressed in military uniforms and civilians." Quoted in David Sapsted, "Millionaire Terrorist Bankrolling War on U.S.," *Daily Telegraph* [Electronic Telegraph Issue 1183], August 21, 1998, 2.

[42]John Norton Moore writes, "Within this intellectual tradition, the role of the international lawyer has been seen as one of seeking to reduce the lawful uses of force, thus progressively constraining the defensive response and increasingly treating both the aggressive attack and the defensive response as equivalent offenses against rational opportunities for diplomacy and third-party legal settlement." "Low-Intensity Conflict and the International Legal System," in Coll, Ord, and Rose, *Legal and Moral Constraints*, 28.

[43]Kaplan, *Strategic Thinking*, 37.

pable of waging unjust wars. All of the implications work in a one-sided manner against those who are required to operate under the doctrine.

The asymmetry of the situation is cause for deep concern. To dismiss it cavalierly, as does Ronald Steel ("We call them 'rogue states' because they are bad places but also because they won't play by our rules"[44]) is to fail to understand the depth and the seriousness of the challenge. To go on, as does Mr. Steel, "We are even debating whether to spend some $60 billion to build a leaky Star Wars umbrella in case one of them is tempted to lob a missile against us. It would probably be cheaper, and safer, to buy off rogue dictators at, say, $1 billion each (and maybe a house in Malibu),"[45] tends to trivialize it. However ironic, this ignores responsibility for the consequences of an attack. The fact remains that the United States cannot tolerate the impact of even a single missile on its territory. Mr. Steel should also have informed his readers how his solution to buy off rogue dictators serves to discourage other rogue dictator "wannabes," or those who fly fuel-laden airliners into skyscrapers.

The principle that customary international law is binding, even though a state has refused to become a party to the agreement that underwrites it, encourages nations to lower their guard. This is a particularly Western notion, not shared universally, and one that might have made some sense in 1945 when the United Nations comprised fifty-one members, most of which were like-minded. The relevance of this idea when there are 190 members of the United Nations—most of which are *not* of the same turn of mind—should, at a minimum, raise a yellow caution flag. The U.S. Department of Defense, in its report on the Gulf War, argued, "Neither is Iraq a party to Hague V, Hague VIII, or Hague IX. However, the provisions of each cited herein are regarded as a reflection of the customary practice of nations, and therefore binding upon all nations."[46] Because there are some legal conventions with which the United States does not agree—parts of Protocol I to the Geneva Conventions of 1949, for example—the United States is reduced to arguments not about the law, but about what is and what is not recognized as customary. Given its questionable and argumentative status, and absent any effort to enforce it, customary international law

---

[44]"The Bad Guys Are Always with Us," *New York Times*, April 30, 2000.

[45]Ibid.

[46]DoD, *Conduct of the Persian Gulf War*, O-2.

must be considered problematic. Nevertheless, its impact on the United States in its planning and use of military force must be considered real and weighty.[47]

Constraints on the use of force inhibit thinking about unconventional threats. If one has no recourse to chemical weapons, to select a nonrandom example, it becomes more difficult to think about the conditions under which an adversary might resort to them. In the same manner, the strongly confining context in which the United States employs all its weaponry reduces its ability to anticipate threats and to fashion the creative use of force to defend against them. Former Secretary of Defense Les Aspin remarked in the spring of 1995:

> We missed what the Soviets thought about nuclear weapons very badly. We asserted that they believed that nuclear weapons are dangerous to both sides, and therefore there is a mutual interest not to use them. . . . But the Russians we now know didn't feel that way. These guys were going to go to nuclear weapons right from the outset—just push the button and away we go. . . . The fact that we didn't have a nuclear war is a real miracle, the likes of which we may never completely understand.[48]

In part, this is a by-product of "attributing to the rest of the world motives, purposes, and modes of behavior similar to [our] own and to ignoring whatever did not fit the pattern. . . . This has been an old established American custom."[49] Often called "mirror imaging," in part, also, it is the result of complacency engendered by confidence in the rule of law. Because one sees only oneself in the mirror, the tilt of the battlespace cannot be observed.

---

[47]For a contemporary discussion of customary law, see Michael Byers, *Custom, Power and the Power of Rules* (Cambridge.: Cambridge University Press, 1999).

[48]Quoted in Joe Williams, "Avoiding Nuclear War Was a 'Miracle,' "*Milwaukee Journal Sentinel,* April 21, 1995, 25. Mr. Aspin "missed what the Soviets thought," and he was in the majority. Others, such as Leon Goure, Foy D. Kohler, and Mose L. Harvey in *The Role of Nuclear Forces in Current Soviet Strategy* (n.p.: Center for Advanced International Studies, University of Miami, 1974), William R. Kintner and Harriet Fast Scott, *The Nuclear Revolution in Soviet Military Affairs* (Norman: University of Oklahoma Press, 1968) and Joseph D. Douglass, Jr., *The Soviet Theater Nuclear Offensive,* Studies in Communist Affairs, Vol. I. Published under the auspices of the U.S. Air Force (Washington, D.C.: U.S. Government Printing Office, 1976)—to cite just three—were listening, fully aware, and writing about it.

[49]Walter Laqueur, "The West in Retreat," *Commentary,* August 1975, 44–45.

The mirror image tends to be very seductive. One finds one's own image quite satisfying. It is easy to say, "I think this way, and others must also." Not much thought or effort is required to accept such platitudes. Evidence to the contrary, of course, is suspect and easy to disown and reject. Consider this in light of the brief discussion above on the subject of the PRC writers' *Unrestricted War.*

Robert Jervis points out that "in the 1930s the British believed that the Germans planned to use air power in the same way that the British did—that is, in strategic attacks on the adversary's homeland. . . . Up to the mid-1970s, the United States thought that Soviet nuclear doctrine resembled American views even though Soviet history, context, and civilian-military relations were very different."[50] The dependence by the Netherlands and Belgium in 1940 on the international law of neutrality was fatal to them. The captain of the USS *Pueblo* in 1968 relied on international law to protect his ship, and he lost it.

The 1972 Biologic and Toxin Weapons Convention has no provisions for verification or for enforcement. Accordingly, "we keep the faith that the simple, declaratory existence of the treaty will help prevent the horrors it describes. Americans sanctify the arms control 'process' as a good in itself, regardless of the strategic situation or the virtue of the treaties under negotiation."[51] In fact, legal arrangements are unable to deal with many interactions between states. Not surprisingly, it is difficult to suggest a single interstate conflict in this century that was conducted strictly in accordance with extant or customary international law. Ironically, the " 'laws of war', *jus in bello,* do imply a rather sophisticated warrior culture in which adversaries are conscious of an overriding common interest in preserving the rules of the game; and it may be precisely this kind of aristocratic society that a war is being fought to destroy."[52] Where the law was effective, states found no reason to violate its provisions. But where the law got in the way, it was often cast aside.

Western states, because the edifice of international law is of their making, have a better record of compliance than others. During its entire history, the Soviet Union, for example, went to war only against

[50]Robert Jervis, "The Drunkard's Search," in *Explorations in Political Psychology,* ed. Shanto Iyengar and William J. McGuire (Durham, N.C.: Duke University Press, 1993), 348, 349.

[51]Steven R. Mann, "Chaos Theory and Strategic Thought," *Parameters* (Autumn 1992): 66.

[52]Howard, "Temperamenta Belli," in Howard, *Restraints on War,* 7.

states with which it had a nonaggression pact. The best that can be said about the international law of armed conflict, however, is that it has been applied unevenly, and its effects have been to tip the battlespace against those who would adhere to its provisions. In fact, there is no evidence to support the contention raised earlier—at least with regard to Western military forces—that "the military . . . would not be inclined to obey the rules that would cause them to lose a war."[53] The evidence lies entirely on the other balance of the scale.

To Western states, the law frequently drives them to seek an operational precision that is unattainable, and which results in paralysis. In stark contrast, nonstate actors operate exclusively outside the reach of international law.

Much like the political correctness movement on college campuses, and the Communist movement before it, constraints on the use of force from a wide variety of sources are being integrated into U.S. strategic culture. As Doris Lessing wrote, "It is not a new thought that Communism debased language and with language, thought. . . . I am not suggesting that the torch of Communism has been handed on to the political correctors. I am suggesting that habits of mind have been absorbed, often without knowing it."[54] The changes are subtle and unobtrusive, yet the effects are wide-ranging.

Take multilateralism, for example. Identified as an organizational constraint on the use of force, it requires all participants to be in agreement to undertake a particular course of action, resulting in a lowest common denominator approach. "Vote" and "veto" are very close, and not only anagrammatically. International forces, according to some commentators, "have to serve a different purpose than do national ones. And sometimes that purpose may be to submit in order to conquer. That is, they may have to forego [sic] combat even at the risk of tactical surrender, all the while striving aggressively for strategic concessions by means of nonviolent tactics, diplomacy, and limited

---

[53]Sandoz, "Preface," in Prokosch, *Technology of Killing*, xiii–xiv.

[54]Doris Lessing, "Unexamined Mental Attitudes Left Behind by Communism," in *Our Country, Our Culture: The Politics of Political Correctness*, ed. Edith Kurzwell and William Phillips (Boston: Partisan Review Press, 1994), 117, 121. Glenn Loury suggested, "It is not the iron fist of repression but the velvet glove of seduction that is the real problem." "Self-censorship," in Kurzwell and Phillips, *Our Country*, 132.

military force."[55] The mind-set is clear here: the means and ways are permitted to dominate the ends. Indeed, as Charles Krauthammer has observed, "The ultimate problem with multilateralism is that if you take it seriously you gratuitously forfeit American freedom of action."[56]

Constraints work their magic on U.S. strategic thought. The central objective more and more has turned to avoiding risks. " 'We've reached the point where the US military doesn't do floors, it doesn't do windows, it doesn't go to war unless the weather is good. It's ludicrous,' said retired Marine Lt. Gen. Bernard Trainor. . . . Risk avoidance appears to have acquired the force of doctrine at the Pentagon."[57] In fact, this is not a new development. In Vietnam, for example, the United States labored under unusual restrictions that reduced its ability both to prosecute the conflict and to protect its forces.[58] But the trends continue over time to hem in the use of force ever more tightly.

Increasingly, the battlespace is tilted away from the strong. Because of all the strictures and constraints placed on the use of force, the United States must enter each potential conflict on an unlevel field. Sometimes, the field is angled in areas that are not thought about very much, such as the use of disinformation. "Don't lie to the press," is a topic fully accepted at all governmental levels today, even—or perhaps especially—if national security is involved. How uniquely Western, and how particularly unhistorical! How quickly the great leverage gained through deception in the Second World War is forgotten![59]

Institutional distrust of the government, an organizational constraint on the use of force, has become acute of late. As Joseph Nye has noted,

[55]Carl Senna, "National Armies and Interests vs. World Armies and Interests," *Providence Journal*, January 10, 1995, A9.

[56]Charles Krauthammer, quoted in Harry G. Summers, *On Strategy II: A Critical Analysis of the Gulf War* (New York: Dell, 1992), 252. One need only recall Prime Minister Chirac's claim with regard to the air action over Kosovo in 1999, "Not a single air strike—and there were about 22,000 of them—was carried out without France's approval," to demonstrate the point. "Chirac Says," *Washington Post*, June 11, 1999, 17. The net result, as retired Admiral Leighton Smith asserted, was to put "our soldiers, sailors, airmen, and Marines at much greater risk. The way Kosovo was executed was Vietnam times 19." Quoted in George C. Wilson, "Kosovo May Be NATO's Last Hurrah," *National Journal*, April 15, 2000.

[57]Chris Black, "US Options Seen Fewer as Military Avoids Risks," *Boston Globe*, July 23, 1995, 12.

[58]See, e.g., Hadley Arkes, *First Things: An Inquiry into the First Principles of Morals and Justice* (Princeton, N.J.: Princeton University Press, 1986), 276.

[59]See, for example, Anthony Cave Brown, *Bodyguard of Lies* (New York: Harper and Row, 1975).

"Trust in the federal government has declined from three-quarters of the public polled in 1970 to less than a quarter today."[60] As the monopolist of military force, the government is obliged to pay a price for this high level of public distrust.

Another of the major effects of the imposition of constraints on the use of force is the loss of flexibility. When threats are free-flowing, unstructured, and ubiquitous—such as terrorism, for example—flexibility must be maximized in order to deal with them. Across the board, constraints depress degrees of freedom to react. Take arms control, for example. Colin Gray puts the issue succinctly:

> In the 1920s and 1930s, and again in the 1970s and 1980s, the side of order quite gratuitously denied itself through arms control some of the flexibility it needed in order to be able to adapt strategically to changing times. Arms control could not and cannot address usefully the security problems that lie in the ambitions and anxieties of would-be revisionist states, but it could and does restrict a policymaker's freedom of action to address the problem with military means.[61]

Insidiously, constraints on the use of force have a way of institutionalizing themselves by influencing preparations for warfare as well. Thus, "Legal norms increasingly set not just the limits of permissible actions, but training and attitudinal parameters as well."[62]

Constraints on training—as on the ability to conduct live firing exercises on the island of Vieques, or at Fort Bragg ("Units must steer clear of 430 red-cockaded woodpecker sites speckled across the 150,000 acre fort"[63]) to cite only two among thousands of examples—render military forces less effective should they have to be used.

---

[60]Joseph Nye, "Home and Abroad," *The National Interest* (Fall 1996): 91.

[61]Gray, *House of Cards*, 104.

[62]Geoffrey Demarest, "The Strategic Implications of Operational Law," Ft. Leavenworth, Kans., Foreign Military Studies Office, April 1995. <http://www.://leav-www.army.mil:80/fmso/lic/PUBS/oplaw.htm> (Accessed March 15, 1997). Cf. "The special solemnity of law is something great powers are often suspicious of. It impedes their freedom of maneuver insofar as it sets up serious constraints." Stanley Hoffman, "Ethics and Rules of the Game between the Superpowers," in *Right v. Might: International Law and the Use of Force*, ed. Louis Henkin, Stanley Hoffman, Jeane J. Kirkpatrick and Allen Gerson, William D. Rogers, and David J. Scheffer, 2nd ed. (New York: Council on Foreign Relations Press, 1991), 73

[63]"Birds Limit Fort Drills, Army Says," Ft. *Worth Star-Telegram*, March 18, 1995, 8

Confusion manifests itself in other ways, such as attempts to ban nuclear weapons, an ingenuous and utopian exercise. Retired Air Force General Charles Horner asserts, "The nuclear weapon is obsolete. I want to get rid of them all. I want to go to zero. I'll tell you why. If we and the Russians can get to zero nuclear weapons, think what that does for us in our efforts to counter the new war. The new war is this [proliferation of] weapons of mass destruction . . . in an unstable world. Think how intolerant we will be of nations that are developing nuclear weapons if we have none. Think of the moral high ground we secure by having none."[64] The roots of this line of thought are complex, but they lie close to an aversion from even the threat of nuclear use.[65]

The timing of this new thrust is rather intriguing. Nuclear weapons have prevented nuclear use very reliably over the past five decades. But precisely when "We can be sure that the time will come when serious and ambitious revolutionaries organize themselves to use mass destruction weapons for realistic political ends, not for clumsy terrorism or self-destructive nihilism,"[66] the cry arises to renounce nuclear weapons and get rid of all of them. The cynicism of the five nuclear members of the United Nations Security Council in their "unequivocal commitment to the ultimate goals of a complete elimination of nuclear weapons,"[67] announced at the sixth review of the Nuclear Nonproliferation Treaty on May 1, 2000, deserves little more than scorn, for it pivots on the definition of "ultimate." Meanwhile, it serves as a political depressant on the value and usefulness of nuclear weapons, especially as a deterrent. Thus, it becomes more and more conceivable that one could have a most powerful grip on the moral high ground, refraining from abhorrent acts or threats, abjuring nuclear weapons, and, in the process, be soundly defeated in a major war. This is yet another example of means and ways

---

[64]Charles Horner, "Horner Advocates Negotiating Elimination of Nuclear Weapons," *Inside the Air Force* 22, July 1994, 12–13; and John Diamond, "Air Force General Calls for End to Atomic Arms," *Boston Globe*, July 16, 1994, 3.

[65]General George Lee Butler, USAF (retired), put it straightforwardly at a press conference to announce the agreement of over sixty top military officers from seventeen countries on dismantling nuclear arsenals: "We simply cannot resort to the very type of act that we rightly abhor." Statement at the National Press Club Newsmaker Luncheon, December 4, 1996 [Electronic Transcript] (Washington, D.C.: Federal News Service, December 4, 1996).

[66]Ikle, "The Next Lenin," 13.

[67]Michael Evans, "Nuclear Powers Pledge to Work towards Disarmament," *London Times*, May 2, 2000.

prevailing over ends. Sight of the ends (defeat) is lost, while the means (no nukes) remain pure.[68]

Nuclear weapons are terrifying. Yet, banning the bomb, in the view of many, would lead to greater insecurity—not increased safety. In this regard, John Mearshimer has written, "Nuclear weapons seem to be in almost everybody's bad book, but the fact is that they are a powerful force for peace. Deterrence is most likely to hold when the costs of going to war are unambiguously stark. The more horrible the prospect of war, the less likely war is."[69] Confusion is rampant. Reportedly, scientists at the Los Alamos National Laboratory have refused to work on nuclear weapon systems except insofar as weapon safety is concerned.[70]

This renewed nuclear aversion continues the trend away from weapons that destroy and kill efficiently to ones that are more and more precise and controlled in their application. Yet, ambivalence prevails, for the enhanced radiation weapon (neutron bomb), which was a very controlled, effective weapon for use against tanks and caused minimal collateral damage, for example, was abandoned for political reasons. The Soviet Union, rather creatively, dubbed it the "Capitalist Bomb," insofar as it destroyed people while leaving capital assets comparatively unscathed. The same was true of nuclear radiation barriers against invasion. Napalm and fuel-air explosives have long been under strong attack as too indiscriminate. As weapons become more accurate, their explosive payload can be reduced and warfare rendered more and more antiseptic.

Given high accuracy and small explosive charges, two contradictory questions will be raised: First, "Doesn't this encourage the use of force rather than make it more difficult?" Thus, "Because wars have become less dangerous to fight, the danger that wars will be fought has increased."[71] Second, "Could not a less violent method been used to

---

[68]The President of Sandia National Laboratories, C. Paul Robinson, has indicated another effect of deep nuclear reductions and an antinuclear mind-set. According to news reports, Mr. Robinson argued that "The United States could wind up aiming its nuclear weapons at huge civilian populations instead of military installations. . . . In this way a smaller nuclear force might paradoxically set the stage for a nuclear war with greater loss of human life." Paul Richter, "U.S. Nuclear Cuts Could Increase Risk to Civilians, Expert Warns," *Los Angeles Times* (Washington Edition), March 28, 1997, 9.

[69]Mearsheimer, "Why," in Betts, *Conflict after the Cold War*, 47.

[70]"No New Nukes," *Aviation Week and Space Technology*, July 22, 1996, 19.

[71]Luttwak, "A Post-Heroic Military Policy," 34.

accomplish the same effect?" A related third question, one high in the minds of military planners, is "To what extent must friendly lives be placed at risk in order to minimize collateral damage?" To an adversary, more accurate weapons with very small warheads might just look like a display of weakness, rather than resolve or discrimination. Then the question might be "Would Saddam Hussein be more impressed by sticking a Tomahawk through the bathroom window of his palace or turning it into a pile of smoking rubble?" This merely rehashes an age-old debate. If war is too terrible to contemplate, that fact can lead either to more humane methods of waging it—thereby making it more likely—or to appeasement or surrender rather than applying the ultimate instrument.

In one clear instance, the U.S. aversion to the use of nuclear weapons spawned nuclear proliferation. The South African acquisition of seven nuclear weapons in the 1980s sought to key South African core security on U.S. nuclear phobia. The South African strategy was not to acquire nuclear weapons to use them against a particular adversary, but, in the time of deadly serious crisis, merely threaten to demonstrate them so that the United States would come to South African assistance in order to avert any nuclear use, even demonstrative. South Africa's leaders judged, probably correctly, that the United States would consider nuclear use of any sort to be worse than efforts expended to come to its aid.[72]

Concern for the nonmilitarization of space, a moral constraint, results in an inability to consider seriously the threat to low-orbit satellites, on which not only U.S. military planning and operations but also the U.S. economy have become very dependent. It has been estimated that "[e]xplosion of a single high-altitude, low-yield nuclear weapon could destroy $14 billion worth of low-earth-orbit satellites that would transit through enhanced radiation belts produced by such a nuclear event."[73] Now, this might not be a threat about which one should be overly concerned. On the other hand, it might be a grave concern, but scant attention is being paid to it because of the irrational regard for not militarizing outer space. Access to space is limited only to those who can

---

[72]See David Albright, "South Africa and the Affordable Bomb," *Bulletin of the Atomic Scientists* 50, 4. LEXIS-NEXIS, Dayton, Ohio: LEXIS-NEXIS (accessed June 13, 1996).

[73]R. C. Webb and others, "The Commercial and Military Satellite Survivability Crisis," *Defense Electronics*, August 1995, 2.

fabricate a booster with sufficient thrust to reach it, or perhaps to those who can merely operate a powerful ground-based laser pointed toward the heavens. In the future, to use space reliably for one's own purposes will require the ability to fight for it.[74] The absence of a determination to secure the use of space, because of constraints imposed, results in yet another tilt in the battlespace.

Shrinking from violent methods and their effects has stimulated a cottage industry in nonlethal or "less-lethal" weapons. Following their appearance on the scene, a debate has risen about their appropriateness and necessity.

Nonlethal means of using force range from acoustic high-frequency bullets and infrasound to biological bacteria to corrode and degrade material to chemicals and microwave generators; and on to the kinetic, optical, and psychotronic.[75] Combustion inhibitors can contaminate fuel or change the viscosity of liquids in devices powered by combustion. Supercaustics can destroy the optics, tires, and structural metals of military vehicles. Antitraction chemicals slicken roads and runways. The list goes on:

> Nonlethal technologies include communications elimination and substitution and other forms of information warfare, various "slickums" and "stickums" to impede vehicle or foot traffic, movement-inhibiting foams and nets to ensnare combatants and vehicles, precision kinetic disabling of heavy weapons, computer-assisted precision anti-mortar/anti-sniper devices, obnoxious sounds or smells that cause flight, counter-sensor lasers, and electronic or electromagnetic means of disabling power grids, communications, computers, and credit networks.[76]

---

[74]The author is indebted to Colin S. Gray for this insight.

[75]"Psychotronic" agents operate on the power of the mind. For example, "The CIA used psychotronics and biocommunication to cause a blood clot in the brain or head of President Saddam Hussein, a procedure that would have obliterated any evidence of the crime, [the newspaper] *Babel* (Baghdad) said on February 13, 1992." "Iraq Accuses U.S. of 'Psychic' Warfare," *Washington Times*, [Reuters], February 14, 1992, A9.

[76]Council on Foreign Relations, *Non-Lethal Technologies: Military Options and Implications*, Report of an Independent Task Force (New York: Council on Foreign Relations, Inc., 1995), 2.

A muddy debate surrounds what nonlethal weapons (NLW) are all about. Some suggest that they can substitute for more deadly means,[77] others that they offer commanders additional options, still others that they add rungs to the escalation ladder. The strongest advocates argue that if less-lethal means are available they must be employed as a matter of humanity. From which point of view, it is only a short stretch to turn the argument normative and argue that as a matter of humanity they *must* be developed and made available. Most of the interest in NLW, however, centers on issues of controlling civilian populations in operations other than war, *not* fighting wars, where—as in the case of riots, for example—deadly force might be inappropriate. Nevertheless, the money that is spent on developing, purchasing, stockpiling, and maintaining NLW cannot be applied to other military purposes, which stands as a genuine economic concern at a time of decreasing defense budgets. Some advocate pursuit of NLW precisely for this reason.

NLW might convey to adversaries or prospective adversaries that their possessors are unwilling to use lethal means.[78] If so, they just might stimulate foul play rather than discourage it. Moreover, they will make rules of engagement, already a knotty topic, even more complicated. Concerns center on their displacing more effective weapons and "on minimizing death, destruction, and suffering not only to noncombatant bystanders (which we already do very well) but to the enemy as well. This makes NLW a questionable deterrent."[79] Those with a visceral passion opposed to the use of force have even raised questions about the legality of some nonlethals, particularly with regard to the Chemical Weapons Convention and the Bacteriological Weapons Convention of 1972.[80]

---

[77]Charles Dunlap, for one, argues, "It would seem prudent then for statesmen and soldiers to view information operations and other 'non-lethal' technologies principally as means to minimize noncombatant casualties under circumstances *where the use of force is otherwise necessary and appropriate*." *Technology and the Twenty-First-Century Battlefield: Recomplicating Moral Life for the Statesman and the Soldier* (Carlisle, Pa.: U.S. Army War College, January 15, 1999), 25. Emphasis in the original.

[78]See Martin N. Stanton, "What Price Sticky Foam?" *United States Naval Institute Proceedings* (January 1996): 58–60.

[79]Martin Stanton, "Nonlethal Weapons: Can of Worms," *United States Naval Institute Proceedings* (November 1996): 60.

[80]See Barbara Rosenberg, " 'Non-lethal' Weapons May Violate Treaties," *The Bulletin of the Atomic Scientists* (September/October 1994): 44–45.

Nonlethal weapons have the effect of making U.S. armed forces more controllable at a time when the speed of warfare demands less centralized control.[81] And they send unfavorable messages to potential adversaries, reinforcing the remarks about deterrence made earlier: "When it sends Marines into danger armed with silly putty and hot pepper, the U.S. government sends a message that they are as concerned about the adversary as about the Americans under their command."[82] In addition, an element of confusion arises when military forces are employed for what is essentially constabulary, or police, work. Former Secretary of Defense Les Aspin made the point well: "If a soldier reacts like a policeman in a military situation, he's dead; if he reacts like a soldier in a police situation, he creates an international incident."[83] So, the legal constraints kick in: "Instead of giving troops another weapon, we will be giving them another way to be second-guessed—another way to bet their stripes, bars, and oak leaves, another way to go to jail."[84]

Required high speeds for military operations—always desirable at the tactical level, but now crucial at the operational and strategic levels as well—cause serious distortions with respect to constraints on the use of force. Rules of engagement cannot deal adequately with fast-moving, information-intensive operations unless they are loosely drawn. Political considerations, however, demand greater and greater control on operations. As a result, "the momentum toward constraining the use of force in so many ways causes a preoccupation with fighting only short, high-tech, low casualty wars," which is "a weakness, not a strength."[85] The remedy for this serious collision between expanding constraints and the need for greater tempo in warfare is not evident.

---

[81]As Jeane Kirkpatrick observed, "A Pentagon briefing on the new non-lethal weapons and the policies governing their use makes clear they are part of the Administration's ongoing campaign to tame American forces." "Sticky Foam and Rubber Bullets," *Baltimore Sun*, March 7, 1995, 9.

[82]Ibid.

[83]Les Aspin, quoted in Karen Eliott House, "The Wrong Mission," *Wall Street Journal*, September 8, 1994, A18.

[84]Stanton, "What Price?" 59.

[85]Grant T. Hammond, "Paradoxes of War," *Joint Force Quarterly* (Spring 1994): 12, 13.

In fact, the effects on military operations of the ever-tightening constraints on the use of force have been to cause hesitation and increase risk.[86] Operationally, it increases the stress on the warfighter. For example, " 'The need for absolute strike accuracy was an extra burden for the pilots,' [General Wesley] Clark said. Each time they prepared to strike, air crews had to think twice about the consequences of missing the target. 'Thinking twice takes time, and that time—those milliseconds or seconds—adds to the risk,' he said."[87]

Another contributor to hesitation is concern over casualties. While the ordinary wisdom on the subject has it that U.S. concern about taking casualties is correlated strongly with the level of U.S. interests at stake, Edward Luttwak writes that suffering casualties is "routinely the decisive constraint," and "present circumstances call for even more than a new concept of war, but for a new mentality that would inject unheroic realism into military endeavor precisely to overcome excessive timidity in employing military means."[88]

Elliot Cohen approaches the issue from a reverse point of view: "[T]he most dangerous legacy of the Persian Gulf War [is] the fantasy

---

[86]One author would view this with alarm: "If the United States chooses to oppose an invasion of an ally, it must do so during the initial states of the attack. Failure to immediately engage the enemy could prove disastrous. If enemy forces gain control of their objective, the US would have to mass forces to expel them." Jeffery R. Barnett, *Future War: An Assessment of Aerospace Campaigns in 2010* (Maxwell Air Force Base, Ala.: Air University Press, January 1996), xxv.

[87]Linda D. Kozaryn, "Serbs Put Up Tough Fight, U.S. Commanders Say," *American Forces Press Service*, June 28, 1999. The "thinking" and its effects was not confined to the missions themselves. If accidents resulted from attacks, "Many [of NATO's aviators] had become demoralized by the accidents and nonstop demands for detailed information about each mishap. Colonels who were supposed to be directing daily missions found themselves reconstructing cockpit video and audio tapes, looking for errors in judgment." Dana Priest, "The Commander's War: Bombing by Committee," *Washington Post*, September 20, 1999, 1.

[88]Luttwak, "Toward Post-Heroic Warfare." Jeffrey Record agrees: "All future U.S. force projection operations will be sternly conditioned by the political imperative of minimizing both U.S. military and enemy civilian casualties—with Desert Storm providing the yardstick by which such operations invariably will be compared. The effects of the casualty minimization imperative in situations not involving supreme U.S. security interests are likely to be pervasive." "Force Projection/Crisis Response," in Ederington and Mazarr, *Turning Point*, 157. Or, as Charles William Maynes has put it, "The West in general has a very large capacity to kill but a very low capacity to die." "The Limitations of Force," in Aspen, *United States Use of Force*, 21. And, as another author writes, "Increasingly, we [Americans] want our wars to be without killing of any sort." Sapolsky, "War without Killing," in Sarkesian and Flanagan, *Domestic and National Agendas*, 27.

of near-bloodless uses of force."[89] But even within this aversion to casualties lies a hidden hierarchy: "The painful reality is that the bombing campaign has been conducted as if the human lives at stake should be priced at three different levels: The most precious lives are those of the NATO pilots, with military tactics explicitly designed to minimize their loss; next are those of Mr. Milosevic's officials, whose headquarters have been targeted only when empty; least valuable are the lives of the Kosovars themselves, on whose behalf no risks have been taken."[90]

This idea that casualties are decisive has its challengers, however. According to Benjamin Schwarz,

> The calculation of many of America's actual and potential adversaries— that the U.S. public is impatient and intolerant of long and costly wars and that, when body bags begin to return to America, the public will respond with demands to withdraw from a conflict—is not supported by the evidence. Although the public can, perhaps, be characterized as impatient, that impatience is far more likely to manifest itself in support for escalating conflict rather than for withdrawing from conflict.[91]

But notice that the "calculation" that's referred to by Mr. Schwarz is what matters. That is the contributor to deterrence and the determinant on which potential adversaries make their decisions. If the perception is as stated, then the reality is comparatively unimportant when it comes to the use of force.

Adversaries are always probing to find weak spots in capability or resolve. They know full well how to take advantage of Western inhibitions. "If the opponents are bloody-minded enough, they will always

---

[89]Eliot A. Cohen, "The Mystique of U.S. Air Power," *Foreign Affairs*, January/February 1994, 121.

[90]Zbigniew Brzezinski, "Compromise over Kosovo Means Defeat," *Wall Street Journal*, May 24, 1999. That this subject can become perverse to the point of being bizarre, here's what the Assistant to the President for National Security Affairs had to say: "Our military technology is so dominant that serious people actually lamented that we did not have enough casualties in the Kosovo conflict." "American Power: Hegemony, Isolationism, or Engagement," Speech at the Council on Foreign Relations, Washington, D.C., October 21, 1999.

[91]Benjamin C. Schwarz, *Casualties, Public Opinion, and U.S. Military Intervention: Implications of U.S. Regional Deterrence Strategies* (Santa Monica, Calif.: RAND, 1994), 24.

exploit the humanitarian attitudes of their adversaries."[92] Consequently, with malice aforethought,

> Weapon production will occur in facilities producing civilian goods. Weapons research activities will be collocated in hospitals, universities, and religious centers. Command and control transmitters and receivers will be placed on schools, hotels, temples, and recreational facilities. Airfields will be joint commercial-military facilities, routinely used by commercial and military entities. . . . An adversary might build tanks in automobile factories, ballistic missiles in refrigerator factories, might comingle military and civilian transport, and could build military garrisons in populous areas.[93]

This asymmetrical approach, of course, has historical precedents: "During the Vietnam War, Hanoi successfully shielded military targets by comingling them with civilian property and cultural objects. Although these actions contravened the law and did not render these targets immune from attack, they remained off-limits to U.S. air strikes."[94] Moreover, the Department of Defense Report, *Conduct of the Persian Gulf War*, made the following relevant observation: "Pronouncements that coalition air forces would not attack populated areas increased Iraqi movement of military objects into populated areas in Iraq and Kuwait to shield them from attack, in callous disregard of its law of war obligations and the safety of its own civilians and Kuwaiti civilians."[95] The global incidence of terrorism on an almost daily basis offers another good

---

[92]James F. Dunnigan, quoted in Dunlap, *Technology and the Twenty-First-Century Battlefield*, 7. Dunlap points out that the Iraqis, Serbs, and Somalis all used human shields. Cf.: "Serbian forces, attempting to flush out ethnic Albanians fleeing Kosovo province, have begun using military helicopters marked with a red cross, refugees said yesterday. . . . With two helicopters high in the sky the one with the red cross moved down to treetop level and fired at us [Elez Elezi] said." Roy Gutman, "From the Air, a Cruel Ruse," *Long Island Newsday*, June 22, 1998. As Bacevich elucidates some of the effects: "Posturing and bravado have superseded resolve, rendering the United States contemptible in the eyes of a tinhorn dictator." Andrew J. Bacevich, "U.S. Emboldens Tinhorn Dictators," *USA Today*, October 22, 1998.

[93]Richard Szafranski, "Parallel War and Hyperwar: Is Every Want a Weakness?" in Barry R. Schneider and Lawrence E. Grinter, eds., *Battlespace of the Future: Twenty-First-Century Warfare Issues*, Air War College Studies in National Security No. 3 (Maxwell Air Force Base, Ala.: Air University Press, September 1995), 139–140.

[94]Humphries, "Operations Law," 34.

[95]DoD, *Conduct of the Persian Gulf War*, O–14.

example of adversaries taking true asymmetrical advantage of the self-constraints of "civilized" states.

Even though the tilt of the battlespace is against the West, a residual concern about "fairness" lingers. Norvell De Atkine and Daniel Pipes report in this regard:

> Scholars barely conceal their anger toward the U.S. military for its part in the Kuwait war; in contrast, they portray Iraqis as misdirected peasants. George Gerbner of the University of Pennsylvania describes how "poorly equipped and demoralized [Iraqi] troops sitting in trenches, caves, bunkers without air cover were napalmed and 'fuel-air bombed' to deprive those inside of oxygen, and then they were bulldozed; dead or alive were buried in some seventy miles of trenches. . . . Defenseless convoys fleeing in panic were bombed and strafed into oblivion in what pilots called a 'turkey shoot.' Edward Said says that the media managed the war to provide "patriotism, entertainment, and disinformation."[96]

This warping of the battlespace results, inter alia, in a reluctance to seek superiority in weaponry, rendering military forces both vulnerable to surprise and preemption, as well as risk averse. Concerns have even been raised, prior to committing and during military use, about the cost and effort of restoring damaged or destroyed enemy material after the conflict.[97]

The moral constraint on blinding lasers has given rise to heated debate. The effect of this constraint is straightforward: one must allow the use of optical sighting against friendly forces. If blinding lasers are taboo, then those who use the sight must be neutralized in other ways. The bottom line is that, instead of injuring the users of optical sights, one is forced—in the name of humanity—to kill them. This is, in a word, bizarre. To go further, however, if one is close enough to use an

---

[96]Norvell B. De Atkine and Daniel Pipes, "Middle Eastern Studies: What Went Wrong?" *Academic Questions* 9, 1 (Winter 1995–1996): 67.

[97]"The cost of economic reconstruction in the Balkans after the Kosovo war could reach $30 billion, according to preliminary European estimates reviewed yesterday by the Group of Seven industrial nations." "Post-War Rebuilding Could Cost $30 Billion, European Officials Say," *Baltimore Sun*, April 27, 1999.

optical sight, then one is very close, indeed. The counterthreat is immi-nent, and that places high stress on the defense. The user of an optical sight knows the imminence of the threat as well, for he must place him-self in a position of jeopardy in order to use the sight. If the other side is known to possess lasers that can blind, what effect will that have on the willingness of the optical sight user to put his eye up to the sight? Thus, deterrence plays a role, and should be considered in the debate. Finally, the power of the laser beam to blind is low compared to the power needed for laser weapons. A tank laser rangefinder, for example, "can burn eyes out to a range of 500 meters, or 2.4 kilometers if the victim is using binoculars."[98] Those who argue the issue on humanitarian rather than operational grounds have enjoyed the upper hand. All voices heard on the humanitarian side, however, have been Western voices.

Advocates for constraints on the use of force seek to make it very difficult to use, to make it truly the *ultima ratio*. They intend to raise the thresholds as high as possible, imposing as many hindrances as possible to a "yes" answer on employing military force. In other terms, only situ-ations that involve national survival or vital national interests, in this view, should merit the use of force. Yet another paradox rears its ugly head, for "wars which are morally compelling or necessary for survival," argues James Payne, "are the ones which should never have to be fought. They are the catastrophes."[99]

A new perspective has arisen that suggests, collectively, that the use of force has outlived its usefulness. Proponents of this line of thought argue either that history has ended with the triumph of democracy (Fukuyama), or that the use of force offers no benefit (Mueller), or that great powers are in eclipse and force cannot prevent their downfall (Kennedy).[100] This is an obvious outcome, and an intended outcome of the myriad constraints on the use of force. The United States is por-

---

[98]Neil Munro, *The Quick and the Dead: Electronic Combat and Modern Warfare* (New York: St. Mar-tin's Press, 1991), 37.

[99]James L. Payne, *The American Threat: The Fear of War as an Instrument of Foreign Policy* (Chicago: Markham Publishing Company, 1970), 223.

[100]Francis Fukuyama, *The End of History and the Last Man* (New York: The Free Press, 1992); John E. Mueller, *Retreat from Doomsday: The Obsolescence of Major War* (New York: Basic Books, 1989); Paul M. Kennedy, *The Rise and Fall of the Great Powers: Economic Change and Military Conflict from 1500 to 2000* (New York: Random House, 1987).

trayed as an enervated, exhausted superpower seeking only comfort in
its transition to old age. Thus:

> The United States and its allies, the states with the greatest interest in
> peace and the greatest power to preserve it, appear to be faltering in
> their willingness to pay the price in money and the risk of lives. Noth-
> ing could be more natural in a liberal republic, yet nothing could be
> more threatening to the peace they have recently achieved.[101]

That "nothing could be more threatening to the peace" is a serious
charge from a serious scholar of the subject.

And so, what has been called the "Clinton Doctrine," described as
"the pre-eminence assigned to casualty avoidance; the emphasis on
holding collateral damage to an absolute minimum; the expectation
that the very prospect of American military action will compel or per-
suade; the unseemly haste to declare even the most modest use (or
threat) of force a roaring success,"[102] represents only one stage, and one
example, of the effects of the multilayered constraints on the use of force
that are reaching a crescendo.

Clearly, the cumulative, corrosive policy effects of all the constraints on the use of force has diluted deterrence and tilted the battlespace, crippling U.S. policy in the past by decision makers taking too little action, or encouraging or requiring them to take the wrong action.
Failure has often been the by-product. In fact, constraints are piled on
willy-nilly, while "the mechanisms by which military effects are supposed to translate into political results are hardly ever studied."[103]

And so, "Robbed of some of our technological edge, slowed by fear
of losses, and timidly proclaiming our desire to limit the damage
inflicted on the enemy, we will find ourselves forced to engage on the
enemy's terms or disengage and go home."[104] The image of the ship of

---

[101]Kagan, On the Origins of War, 572.

[102]Andrew J. Bacevich, "Policing Utopia: The Military Imperatives of Globalization," The National
Interest (Summer 1999): 6.

[103]Robert A. Pape, Bombing to Win: Air Power and Coercion in War (Ithaca, N.Y.: Cornell University Press, 1996), 328.

[104]Mark J. Conversino, "Sawdust Superpower: Perceptions of U.S. Casualty Tolerance in the Post-
Gulf War Era," Strategic Review (Winter 1997): 22.

state sinking beneath the waves, its sword firmly sheathed but its captain standing tall saying, "I did the right thing," recurs, and it is truly a chilling image to those who believe in the ultimate correctness of the American experiment. What the United States lacks, and has lacked for some time, is what James Payne has called "a tradition of debate which protects us against the evil consequences of a failure to use force."[105]

---

[105]Payne, *American Threat*, 222.

CHAPTER 6

Remedies

Twice armed is he that has his quarrel just
But best of all is he that gets his blow in fust.

F.S. Northedge

We don't want any fair fights.

General Michael E. Ryan

If causes and effects are complex, then remedies cannot be simple. The first difficulty in finding and implementing a remedy arises with the appreciation that the problem has not been recognized. Operational strictures are grounded in an interest in using only the amount of force necessary to accomplish objectives without assuming inordinate risks. Organizational constraints are imposed to limit the relative power of the various organs that are required to work together. Legal and arms control constraints arise from the mutual interest of states in controlling the violence and damage caused by armed forces, especially in their effects on noncombatants, and in controlling military expenditures. Moral constraints arise from humanitarian concerns that, on balance, the use of force be for "good" or "right" purposes only and that outcomes not offend moral sensibilities. From the U.S. point of view, virtually all constraints have been adopted willingly and purposefully. But if the effects detailed in the preceding chapter are accurate—deterrence is weakened and the battlefield is tilted unfavorably, the potential results bordering on catastrophic—then the situation is grave, and concern should be increasing.

As is well-known, the North Koreans possess chemical and biological weapons. They have worked on nuclear weapons; whether they possess operational weapons of mass destruction (WMD) remains a matter of debate at this juncture. They have demonstrated ballistic missile delivery capability covering the entire Korean peninsula and reaching the Japanese islands. A Democratic People's Republic of Korea (DPRK) army numbering over half a million men is bivouacked near the demilitarized zone. The United States maintains about 37,000 troops in Korea, but are these soldiers a tripwire or a sacrificial force? If the troops were not already deployed to the Korean peninsula, would the United States undertake and sustain such a commitment today? If war were to break out, would the North Koreans refrain from using their WMD? Is the United States prepared to use nuclear weapons preemptively against the DPRK in order to save its troops? If the answers to these two latter questions are both "no," then the force is sacrificial. Is the United States truly prepared today to sacrifice up to 37,000 of its fighting men and women for the security of South Korea? Alternatively, are there remedies that might be taken that would change the situation so that it becomes clear that U.S. soldiers in South Korea are not sacrificial? Nobody knows what the leaders of the DPRK will do. Consequently, in this scenario, the prospective "regret factor" appears very high.

The Korean example typifies how shallow the thinking runs. So hemmed in are the available options by constraints on the use of force that the question of the sacrificial force languishes, unaddressed. If it were addressed seriously, some remedies would surely be forthcoming. But the implied constraints suppress remedial thought and perpetuate the potential for deep, heartrending regret.

The Korean example is a straightforward one that encompasses potential cross-border aggression. In the vast majority of cases, however, according to Alberto Coll, "The traditional rules of international law and the legal framework of the United Nations Charter, elaborated to deal with outright, open conventional military aggression, are difficult to apply to the highly creative modes of violence characteristic of 'violent peace' and unconventional warfare."[1] Coll goes on to argue: "Any serious study of unconventional warfare and the perils it poses to liberal democracies in the late twentieth century will have to go beyond the realm of international law and organization and consider the wider range of policy responses available to democratic States, including some forms of unconventional warfare itself."[2] By both design and effect, con-

---

[1] Alberto R. Coll, "Unconventional Warfare, Liberal Democracies, and International Order," in Coll, Ord, and Rose, *Legal and Moral Constraints*, 4.

[2] Ibid., 19.

straints on the use of force narrow the range of policy responses. Perhaps, as Coll implies, the United States will have to reach outside international law and organizations for remedies.[3]

Rather than taking action to prepare the country to deal with new potentialities, the United States continues to pursue actions in each of the four areas to *increase* the level of constraint on the use of force, thereby demonstrating even further that the problems they pose and the regrets they promise have not yet been recognized. Eliot Cohen, some years ago, asserted that "[t]he American government needs to prepare itself, materially, organizationally, and psychologically, for the day after the first nuclear weapon is used in anger."[4] But just the opposite has eventuated. One is reminded on a daily basis that many of the restraints are anachronistic at best, harmful to national security at worst. In fact, the security environment in which these constraints have grown over time has changed significantly. The context in which they were adopted has altered, but they have not been modified to fit the new context. Adda Bozeman offers four ways in which the world has changed that bear on the subject at hand:

1. The states system has ceased to be what it used to be between the Groatian seventeenth century and our twentieth century.

2. Our understandings and definitions of "war" are hopelessly out of date, and the same holds, *mutatis mutandis*, for "peace."

3. The international law of war is basically irrelevant today, and I doubt it can become relevant again.

4. "National security" can no longer be calculated and rendered in terms of military preparedness and treaty provisions.[5]

---

[3]An excellent example of this was the establishment of military tribunals at the end of World War II and again in the Afghanistan campaign in the war against terrorism (Operation Enduring Freedom). Such special courts offer a way to deal with unlawful combatants—those who operate outside the accepted laws of armed conflict—and thereby relinquish legal protections that they might claim as, for example, prisoners of war. Tribunals constitute a special measure necessarily to deal with acts and situations outside the reach of normal civil law or even the laws of armed conflict.

[4]Eliot Cohen, "Three Comments," *The National Interest* (Winter 1993–1994): 37. To allow that the September 11, 2001, attacks used weapons of mass destruction would be to say that, in principle, this has already happened.

[5]Adda B. Bozeman, "U.S. Conceptions of Democracy and Security in a World Environment of Culturally Alien Political Thought: Linkages and Contradictions," in Sarkesian and Flanagan, *U.S. Domestic and National Agendas*, 55.

A sensible extension of Professor Bozeman's observation is that control over WMD has devolved to individuals, rather than states. If Professor Bozeman is anything like close to the mark, many of the constraints detailed in previous chapters are not only misplaced, but could be very counterproductive. Edward Luttwak offers this observation: "Once more, as in centuries past, wars are rather easily started and then fought without perceptible restraint. When belligerents see that no particular penalty is paid for opening fire first or using any and all means of warfare—even the wholesale destruction of cities by aerial or artillery bombardment—self-imposed restraints on the use of force are everywhere eroded."[6] But Luttwak is not thinking about the United States. He's thinking about Iran and Iraq, perhaps, but what other post-World War II "wars" were fought "without perceptible restraint"? And what "self-imposed restraints" on the United States were "everywhere eroded" in Vietnam, the Gulf War, or Kosovo?

Professionals talk to themselves about the problem, but general familiarity is lacking. Just before his death, Les Aspin remarked, "Because we no longer have the draft, many Washington power brokers have no experience of what the military's all about. The White House staff is unfamiliar with the military. Each Congress becomes less familiar. The same holds true for the press corps—almost anywhere you look here there's a diminishing pool of people with military experience."[7] From Chechnya to Albania to Rwanda and back to Lebanon and over to Myanmar and Indonesia, the evidence is abundant, but unrecognized in the terms outlined here.

This is not to argue that the United States should intervene or use military force in Chechnya, Myanmar, or Tibet. That is not the thesis. Rather, the contention is that if U.S. interests were to become jeopardized in any of those places (or by terrorists based, grown, or trained there), and if it became evident that military force might be called for in response, the United States would have neither the wherewithal nor the stomach (capability or will) to respond in a manner that was timely, correct, or adequate. That there was no timely response to the bombing of the USS *Cole* in Aden, Yemen, in November 2000 is not simply a

---

[6]Luttwak, "Toward Post-Heroic Warfare," 109.

[7]Quoted in Charles Peters, "Tilting at Windmills," *Washington Monthly* (September 1995): 4.

matter of poor intelligence and low readiness. It is also a function of the need to provide "lawyer's proofs" in order to justify the use of force.[8] Recall the domestic and international calls for hard evidence of Osama bin Laden's involvement in the September 11, 2001, attacks before military force was employed in Afghanistan.

The danger is real. Interstate conflict continues, and animosities fester. Terrorism lives, and, because of its nature, must be attacked both on the state and individual levels in an open-ended effort. The urgency of seeking remedies is rubricated by the fact that the asymmetrical capability for causing irreparable harm continues to grow and shows no clear signs of abating.

> Crude designs for nuclear, chemical, and biological weapons are increasingly available in book form and on the Internet. . . . Closer to home, extremists and cults are experimenting with weapons of mass destruction. . . . A convincing inventory of nuclear materials has yet to be taken in Russia, and the inventory system for warheads is still not up to par. With respect to nuclear material, a Russian Security Council official has said that as much as 10 percent of inventory was hidden away during the Soviet period to be prepared to meet five-year plans. Now the Russian government has no idea where that hidden inventory is located.[9]

The effects of the myriad of constraints cause decision makers to act with benefit neither of experience nor anticipation. Deterrence is undermined daily, and the battlespace becomes ever more skewed. Each problem is approached de novo, but the burden of constraint weighs down options for solution. Decision makers act emotionally, unable to

---

[8]Cf. "Clinton's speech [February 17, 1998], designed to elaborate a casus belli turned into a lesson in contract law: Saddam made a promise (to give up weapons of mass destruction) and 'now, instead of playing by the very rules he agreed to at the end of the Gulf War, Saddam has spent the better part of the past decade trying to cheat on this solemn commitment.' Fire away. This is the kind of legalistic war rationale that an undersecretary of defense might offer to the World Affairs Council of Northern California. But a president? Rallying the nation? It represents a most depressing reprise of that stereotypical liberal obsession: international relations as process—rules, commitments, contracts, resolutions, promises, signatures, parchment." Charles Krauthammer, "Listless War Cry . . . ," *Washington Post*, February 19, 1998, 17.

[9]Jessica Stern, "Terrorism Multiplied," *Washington Post*, July 17, 1996, 19.

divorce the affairs of state from their own personal affectations, mes-
merized by the mirror image. As George Will has written, "Soothing
assumptions about the good faith and shared interests of antagonists are
natural to democracies, as is the desire to spend money on things other
than defense. Getting a democracy to do what does not come naturally
requires leadership."[10] So, there's a case to be made for leadership as
one ingredient for whatever constitutes a remedy. The actions post-
September 11 by the administration of George W. Bush offer an object
lesson in this regard.

Leadership must be exercised on behalf of a goal, however. And in
conflict, one must care—one must care passionately—who prevails. To
be neutral or agnostic on key issues of national interest is to forfeit a
voice in critical matters of action. In order to support many of the constraints that have been placed on the use of force in the United States,
one would have to take a position devoid of partisanship. That is, one
would have to argue that the use of force, or a particular weapon, was
improper or immoral in and of itself, regardless of the user. Stopping the
fighting would take precedence over winning.[11]

To put it another way, one would have to be indifferent to the outcome so long as some rule or principle was not violated. Or, the ends
would be subservient entirely to ways and means. Many of the constraints issue from this mind-set: if we should lose a war because of this
particular constraint, that's the price we should be willing to pay because
the constraint is so intrinsically good and valuable in itself. But, as Colin
Gray reminds us, it is not weapons, but who owns them that matters:
"Clear military advantage on the side of order is a force for peace. . . .
For an extreme example, an Iraqi ICBM force would not be the same as
the U.S. ICBM force, no matter how similar the two forces might be in
their technical characteristics and standard practices of operation."[12]

---

[10]George F. Will, "Soothing Assumptions," *Washington Post,* June 27, 1996, 29.

[11]With regard to nuclear weapons, this is the thesis of Leon Weiseltier in "When Deterrence Fails,"
Foreign Affairs, Spring 1985, 827–847.

[12]Gray, *House of Cards,* 78. See also his *Weapons Don't Make War: Policy, Strategy, and Military
Technology* (Lawrence: University Press of Kansas, 1993). Churchill appreciated the point also, as
he "unhesitatingly endorsed the Western monopoly of the atomic bomb, emphasizing his opposition to entrusting U.S. and British knowledge of its secrets to the U.N. 'It would be criminal madness to cast it adrift in this still agitated and un-united world,' he warned. No country had slept less
well because the secrets of the bomb were held in American hands, but this would not have been
the case had 'some Communist or neo-Fascist State monopolised for the time being these dread
agencies.' " Quoted in Warren, "Churchill's Realism," 39.

Thus, ends must be weighed as well as means and ways. Ends, ways, and means must all be brought into harmony. Means may have to be adjusted to serve the right ends. Michael Howard offers food for thought:

> War . . . involves inherent constraints. It is carried out by men making conscious choices and obedient to hierarchical commands. . . . Orders can be given to spare as well as to destroy. Whatever the objective aimed at or the weapons used, the plea of military necessity has to be brought into focus with two other requirements, arising from the nature of man as a moral and as a social being. The first imposes an ethical rule: one does not cease to be a moral being when one takes up arms, even if required by military necessity to commit immoral acts. There are other tribunals to which one may be called to account. And the second imposes a prudential rule: one should not behave to one's adversary in such a way as to make subsequent reconciliation impossible. War is instrumental, not elemental: its only legitimate object is a better peace.[13]

Thomas Jefferson had it just right: "To lose our country by a scrupulous adherence to written law, would be to lose the law itself, with life, liberty, property and all those who are enjoying them with us; thus absurdly sacrificing the end to the means."[14]

Practical application of this was no more clear than the bombing campaign of the Second World War. As Williamson Murray put it: "The combined bomber offensive . . . did lead to the death of civilians. And it did not reach the over-optimistic goals which its advocates had intended. But the bomber offensive was essential to winning the war in Europe. . . . There was nothing pretty or redeeming about the effort itself; but there was no other choice."[15] In other words, the means had to be adjusted in order to accomplish the right ends.

---

[13]Howard, "Temperamenta Belli," in Howard, *Restraints on War*, 13–14.

[14]In an 1810 letter to J. B. Colvin, quoted in Robert F. Turner, "State Sovereignty, International Law, and the Use of Force in Countering Low-Intensity Aggression in the Modern World," in Coll, Ord, and Rose, *Legal and Moral Constraints*, 44. Jefferson's referral was to *written* law. On the drawbacks and dangers of *customary* international law, see, for example, George Galdorisi, "It's Time to Sign On," *United States Naval Institute Proceedings*, January 1998, 51–53.

[15]Williamson Murray, "The Meaning of World War II," *Joint Force Quarterly* (Summer 1995): 54–55.

States and substate groups, for reasons of their own, act in ways contrary to international law and violate the constraints that have been illuminated herein. Aggression and genocide—ethnic cleansing in the Balkans, the conflicts in Chechnya and Kashmir, and the Hutu/Tutsi bloodletting in Africa—offer only the most recent examples.

Given dire circumstances, to what extent can constraints be violated or ignored? Would torture of a terrorist who had knowledge of a biological warfare plot to kill hundreds of thousands of persons be allowed? Indeed, Israel's Supreme Court has ruled that torture is permissible against Islamic extremists in some situations.[16] This raises the question of "dirty hands," the idea that sometimes the exercise of statecraft requires immoral acts. Or as Ronald Steel puts it, "If one's enemy is absolutely evil (as he usually is, by definition), then any means used against him becomes moral."[17] Adjustments, in fact, have been made: "The intelligence officer of the U.S. Fifth Air Force declared on July 21, 1945, that 'the entire population of Japan is a proper military target,' and he added emphatically, *'There are no civilians in Japan.'* "[18]

The issue, however, need not be so stark: "It is a paradox of the principle of balance of power," wrote Hedley Bull in 1977, "that while the existence of a balance of power is an essential condition of the operation of international law, the steps necessary to maintain the balance often involve violation of the injunctions of international law."[19] Some argue that "dirty hands" cannot be tolerated: "There are hands so dirty that we should not use them to win a war. There are wars that should not be fought and wars that should not be won. The moral hope, of course, is to fight only those that should be won."[20] But can leaders base security policy solely on hope? Should the lives and welfare of millions be dependent on the hope that only the wars that can be won will be fought—or, should be fought?[21]

---

[16]"Israeli Court Allows Coercion," *Washington Times*, November 16, 1996, A-5.

[17]Steel, *Temptations*, 93.

[18]Paul Fussell, *Thank God for the Atom Bomb and Other Essays* (New York: Summit Books, 1988), 27. Emphasis in the original.

[19]Hedley Bull, *The Anarchical Society* (London: Macmillan Press, 1977), 108.

[20]Sidney Axinn, *A Moral Military* (Philadelphia: Temple University Press, 1989), 150.

[21]"CHORUS: Hast not more boldly in aught else transgressed?
PROMETHEUS: I took from man expectancy of death.
CHORUS: What cure did you provide them with against that sickness?
PROMETHEUS: I planted blind hope in the heart of him." Aeschylus, *Prometheus Bound*, *Library of the Future*, 4th ed., (Las Vegas, Nev.: World Library, Inc., 1999), CD.

Indeed, rationalizations can be found even with regard to Mutual Assured Destruction, the mutual threat to kill many noncombatants in retaliation for a nuclear attack. Here's what George Quester has written on that subject: "My own favorite outcome might be a frank and honest acceptance of the contingent moral logic of mutual assured destruction, by which threats to civilians are justified when they prevent or end wars. Short of that I would prefer more hypocritical sliding into such an acceptance . . . rather than accept any philosophically honest pursuit of alternatives that made war more likely."[22] For Quester, the threat to kill millions of noncombatants is justified because in his judgment it makes war less likely. This is an excellent example of the powerful numbing effect that accompanies the great number of restraints that have been uncritically accepted. All thought about creative ways to regulate conflict without restricting the use of force is snuffed out. What Professor Quester does not look squarely in the eye is the fact that an alternative exists to the levy of such an immoral threat: effective strategic defenses. Unless he is prepared to sustain an argument that strategic defenses make war more likely, Quester's option appears unsustainable. The existence of the alternative invalidates his choice. Given a real choice, why should one opt for amorality?

So, what will happen? One prophetic projection contended that "state-sponsored terrorism remains the number one danger. Iraq, Iran, Syria, Sudan, Libya, and North Korea are pariahs for good reason. If their support for terrorism is not ended, the chances are that sooner or later a truly horrific event will occur. Predictably, at that point, Congress will take the subject seriously, and we will worry less about how proposed antiterrorist legislation intrudes on our civil rights and more about how it assures our physical security."[23] Similarly, "The day will come when we will not be able to meet a major military challenge. That does not appear to worry us. When that happens, we will do what English speaking peoples have done for the last 300 years. We back up, triple defense budgets, and kill thousands of our youth before getting it all sorted out again."[24] Can't a better way be found to meet these foreseeable difficulties? Must it be necessary, because of a lack of vision, to forfeit the rights of the innocent rather than employ force against the guilty?

---

[22]Quester, "Necessary Moral Hypocrisy," in Shue, *Nuclear Deterrence*, 269.

[23]Geoffrey Kemp, letter to the editor, *The National Interest* (Summer 1996): 125.

[24]Dov Zakheim, "Preparing for a World to Unravel," ROA *National Security Report*, August 1995, 35.

Once U.S. leaders come to grips with the fact that there is a problem, if they

- accept the fact that ends, ways, and means must be balanced—that
  there are no absolute answers in the choices that must be made
  among them;

- forsake the mirror image—the uncritical assumption that others
  think precisely and will act as the United States does;

- understand that hope cannot be the foundation for policy; and

- reconcile the moral difference between actions of the state and
  interpersonal acts,

then they can take the next step in resolving the problem: to specify
carefully for themselves the conditions under which the use of force is
absolutely necessary. This specification will shape the strategic culture.
It will establish limits on the range of constraints on the use of force that
are acceptable. It cannot bend to the current cultural norms, for they are
already captured by the restrictions. The cases will be few, not many:
"We can't lead if we don't put our own people at risk, but few of these
postmodern crises offer the sort of compelling moral strategic appeal
that Presidents traditionally use to justify putting American soldiers in
harm's way."[25]

The Weinberger Doctrine was an important step in the right direction, but it was unduly confining, and dealt exclusively with *jus ad bellum* and not *jus in bello*.[26] What's more, the tenets of the Weinberger

---

[25]Thomas L. Friedman, "The No-Dead War," *New York Times*, August 23, 1995, 21.

[26]"Weinberger's six tests, designed to resolve the question of when to commit military forces, appear
to create more problems than they solve and raise false hopes by offering easy solutions to complex
problems. In the first place, the Weinberger tests institutionalize the need to have popular support
(actually popular enthusiasm) for a war. It ignores the fact that some strategically necessary wars and
causes may be unpopular. Second, the Weinberger tests appear to define winning in the traditional
American fashion. Limited war or simply achieving the limited goals of a superpower is not satisfying in the American approach to war. Third, the Weinberger tests give lip service to assessing both
national interest and clearly defined political and military objectives prior to committing U.S. military forces. Both before and after the publication of the six tests, however, the current administration has produced a long list of objectives and interests so diffuse that not even the enormous Soviet
military establishment could hope to cover all the commitments it has undertaken. Finally, going to
war only as a last resort is not a new policy, developed through the Weinberger tests. It is traditionally American." Samuel J. Newland and Douglas V. Johnson II, "The Military and Operational Significance of the Weinberger Doctrine," *Small Wars and Insurgencies* 1, 2 (August 1990): 186–187.

Doctrine might have been useful in that place at that time, but a fresh appraisal is needed today by today's leaders.

Understanding would start with an appreciation that one must plan to act against capabilities, but to deter intentions. It should not be particularly difficult to draw up a list of adversarial actions that would cause U.S. leaders to be forced to confront a decision on whether or not to use force to deal with them. Some acts taken against the United States, for example, clearly should result in a declaration of war.[27] Importantly, moreover, declarations of war need not be aimed at other states:

> Declarations of war traditionally have been directed against nation-states, but now terrorist groups deliberately eschew national identity, creating a loophole in international law through which, until recently, they could wage war with relative impunity. A formal declaration of war by the United States would not only eliminate that subterfuge, but restore symmetry to the battlefield. . . . Peace cannot be preserved if those who declare war against us are allowed to do so without their own survival placed in jeopardy.[28]

Even though the option has not been used since 1945, declaring war brings with it an array of privileges and obligations. Below the level of a declaration of war, one might "declare a crisis," or "declare a contingency," which would, coincidentally, open up a set of options that might be adopted at that level of declaration. Options withheld at the level of "contingency" would be made available at higher levels of concern. A graduated system for decision making might be crafted in

---

[27]On April 13, 1999, just three weeks into the 78-day bombing campaign over Kosovo, the *Wall Street Journal* called for the U.S. Congress to declare war, arguing that "Congress can make its best contribution if it focuses on the goals, and not merely the means, of a Balkans war. Force can of course be used for limited aims as long as we understand what they are. But we are now beyond that point with nationalistic passions once again loose in Europe, 500,000 refugees, and U.S. and NATO air forces already deeply engaged. Senator McCain's suggestion of a resolution urging 'all means necessary' to win is to the point. Congress should declare war for the right reasons, and America should use whatever forces are necessary to achieve those goals as quickly and decisively as possible." Editorial, "Declare War," *Wall Street Journal,* April 13, 1999, 18. There were many calls for the Congress to declare war after the September 11, 2001, attacks.

[28]Harry Summers, "Noli me Tangere . . . With Congressional Support," *Washington Times,* August 26, 1998, 17

which, at certain levels of threat or indicated activity by an adversary or potential adversary, some particular decisions would be forthcoming.[29] For the purpose of increasing readiness and reducing the possibility of surprise, the U.S. military has a system of "defense conditions" (DEFCONs) that call for a range of actions as each particular condition is set. The last time a DEFCON was set, however, was in 1979.[30]

A policy of "anticipatory self-defense," discussed briefly in Chapter 2, would take a step in the direction of dealing both with adversarial capabilities and intentions. If an adversary, or potential malefactor, knew that such a policy was in place, it might be deterred from contemplating or preparing for an attack. While controversial, such a policy might be adopted merely because the consequences of accepting or absorbing an attack might be dire. If it became known, for example, that a terrorist cell was manufacturing biotoxins and intended to disseminate them in the center of a large city, should not an anticipatory attack be considered, given the potential loss of innocent lives that could result? Can the inherent ambiguities in such a situation be reduced so that action can be taken without excessive hesitation and with strong reservations? Time might well be of the essence, and as the potential for the acquisition and use of WMD becomes more widespread, pressures will mount to make this a live policy issue.[31]

Because deterrence depends fundamentally on the credibility of both a willingness to take strong measures and the means to do so, adopting a posture that makes the declaration of war a less-encumbered option or developing and publicizing a doctrine for anticipatory self-defense would take strides to shore up the "willingness" side of the deterrence calculus. As Grant Hammond has argued, "Often it is only by

---

[29]In keeping with his preoccupation with casualty avoidance, Edward Luttwak has suggested a "ranking of usability" for U.S. military force beginning with unmanned long-range weapons and ending with "the least usable forces with the largest combat echelons." Edward N. Luttwak, "The Crisis of Classic Military Power and the Possible Remedy of 'Post-Heroic' Intelligence-Based Warfare," in *The Information Revolution and International Security*, Henry Ryan and C. Edward Peartree (Washington, D.C.: The CSIS Press, 1998).

[30]Belatedly, the government has begun to move down this path by a new system of alerts—but not of anticipatory acts or responses. See, for example, August Gribbin, "White House Seeks Graduated Terrorism Alerts," *Washington Times*, January 13, 2002, 13.

[31]A discussion of the question of "legitimate anticipation" appeared in Richard N. Haass, "Military Force: A User's Guide," *Foreign Policy* 96 (Fall 1994): 21–37.

demonstrating a willingness to go to war that the requirement to do so can be avoided."[32]

Means, the other component of deterrence, must be reassessed as well. Some years ago, Bernard Brodie articulated the issue in this manner: "Regardless of how impregnable our defenses are, and they can never be perfectly so, our security in the world is jeopardized if we cannot inflict vital injury on any nation which menaces us or our legitimate interests."[33] Perhaps a reordering of the means of fighting might alleviate the problem. For example, would it not be sensible to place robots "in harms way," and to have unmanned machines offer up their lives for the cause rather than U.S. fighting troops? Instead of soldiers slugging it out at close range, might not an effort be made to achieve one's ends from long range by means of senior citizens firmly clicking computer mice? Can the argument be resurrected that it is immoral to absorb a first hit—especially with WMD—rather than to prevent it through anticipatory action?

Notice, however, that the DEFCON system and the schemes sketched briefly in the paragraph above lie wholly within the currently imposed constraints on the use of force. The arrangement proposed here, on the other hand, would—with a clear eye fixed on the balance between ends, ways, means, and risks—systematically overturn selective constraints as a matter of necessity. How else can those asymmetrical threats, those threats developed in anticipation of constraints preventing preemption or adequate response, be sensibly addressed in the future?

One way to bypass many of the constraints levied on the use of military force is simply to hire mercenaries. This approach has the benefit, inter alia, of not exposing one's own troops to the possibility of returning home in body bags. Mercenaries have been employed throughout recorded history. The observation, for example, was made that after Japan had contributed to the 1991 Gulf War, the coalition acted as Japan's mercenaries, protecting Japanese access to the Persian Gulf oil

---

[32]Grant T. Hammond, "Paradoxes of War," *Joint Force Quarterly* (Spring 1994): 14. Or, as Herman Kahn wrote in his seminal work, "Usually the most convincing way to look willing is to be willing." Herman Kahn, *On Thermonuclear War* (Princeton, N.J.: Princeton University Press, 1960), 287.

[33]Bernard Brodie, *A Layman's Guide to Naval Strategy* (Princeton, N.J.: Princeton University Press, 1943), 6.

trove.[34] By employing mercenaries, the United States would "simply admit that we have no choice but to equip and fund, at arm's length, a bunch of professional volunteer soldiers drawn from many nations who are prepared to fight where we are not."[35] Yet, it seems fair to ask, "Is this the courageous path for U.S. statecraft of the future?"

Mercenaries, notwithstanding, as an option, having a set of guidelines for the use of force in a complete set of contexts, thought through in advance, will help illuminate the constraints on the use of force and to reduce their effects. It will identify those constraints that must be rolled back; to date, the assumption has been that constraints can only increase, that there was a ratchet effect preventing their reversal. It will highlight constraints from which relief must be sought. It will bring to the forefront those situations in which "dirty hands" choices must be made and offer possibilities for negating them before they arise. It will highlight the requirements for immediate or specific deterrence by focusing on the conditions under which the use of force would be required.

A set of guidelines for the use of force will make clear the fact that the less vital the interest, the less obvious the requirement for the use of force, the more carefully integrated the political and military efforts must be so that both risks and unintended consequences can be better controlled. It will help illustrate those situations in which a symmetrical, or proportionate, response will be considered by the adversary to be a show of weakness[36] that merely stimulates him to greater adverse activity.

It might well illustrate the value and the importance of targeting the adversary's leadership as an effective and efficient way to bring a conflict

---

[34]"Large financial contributions from Saudi Arabia, Kuwait, the United Arab Emirates, Japan, Germany, South Korea, and others [helped] defray U.S. incremental costs. The total amount committed to defray the cost of U.S. involvement in the war was almost $54 billion. This spread the financial burden of the war and helped cushion the U.S. economy from its effects." United States, Office of the Secretary of Defense, *Conduct of the Persian Gulf Conflict: Report to Congress*, July 1991, xi–xii.

[35]In this way, "We can admit that, like Rome and Florence, we have become plump and squeamish with wealth." Frederick Forsyth, "Send in the Mercenaries," *Wall Street Journal*, May 15, 2000. See also Michael Kinsley, "Mercenaries: Why Not?" *Washington Post*, May 30, 2000, 19.

[36]"In the past, finding the guilty would lead to some tit-for-tat 'proportionate' retaliation on the offending country, such as Clinton's risible cruise missile attack on Iraq—on empty offices in the middle of the night—for the 1993 assassination plot on George Bush. Such perfunctory responses are a declaration of unseriousness." Charles Krauthammer, "Declare War on Terrorism—Literally," *Washington Post*, August 9, 1996, 17.

to termination.[37] It will force decision makers to confront those situations in which the consequences of conforming to the constraints will be more devastating than departing from them. It will have to come to grips with the suggestion that "[a] military force is fundamentally anti-humanitarian: its purpose is to kill people in the most efficient way possible."[38] It will open eyes to the fact that in the United States military actions have been narrowly circumscribed to reactions to acts based on a standard of proof that is close to that required in U.S. criminal courts. By opening a channel to counter those severe, truly asymmetrical threats, it will point out the extent to which many of the constraints are strictly fair weather phenomena: When the going gets tough, the constraints get going.[39]

---

[37]"To judge by the declarations of both sides in connection with events in the Gulf, the idea that rulers should not enjoy immunity but be held personally accountable for their actions and liquidated if necessary is spreading. Growing out of the dark recesses where terrorists and counterterrorists meet each other, it has begun to extend to interstate conflict. A foreglimpse of such a state of affairs was provided not only by the Gulf War but also by the American attempt to bomb Libya's Gadhafi in his bed and the rather more successful kidnapping of Panamanian dictator Noriega. Whether these tendencies will be contained, or whether we are heading toward a return to the standards of an earlier time when there was no distinction between ruler and state and the waging of war ad hominem was the rule—only time will tell." Van Creveld, "Persian Gulf Crisis," 33. With regard to the 1999 Kosovo action, Jacob Sullum wrote, " 'Although NATO sent a missile into Mr. Milosevic's bedroom,' the New York Times dryly reported, 'officials insisted that it was nothing personal.' This stance reflects a perverse policy that forbids the assassination of foreign political leaders, even those guilty of mass murder, yet sanctions the slaughter of innocent noncombatants as unavoidable 'collateral damage.' . . . Writing in the May 17 New Republic, historian Daniel Jonah Goldhagen suggests that we need not feel too bad about this situation because the Serbs deserve to suffer. 'Any people that commits imperial war, perpetrates wholesale murder and assaults entire peoples—not just their armies but unarmed men, women, and children—has forfeited the protections that the norms and conventions of sovereignty usually afford.' . . . Would it be fair to say that every American is morally responsible for the consequences of this campaign?" Jacob Sullum, "Mantle of Collective Guilt," Washington Times (May 17, 1999), A17. A somewhat novel way to dodge the stricture on assassination might be contained in the words of Senator Orrin Hatch, "who has suggested U.S. laws be changed to allow the assassination of known terrorists." Harry Summers, "Wanted Dead or Alive," Washington Times, August 18, 1998, 18.

[38]Samuel P. Huntington, "New Contingencies, Old Roles," Joint Force Quarterly (Autumn 1993): 43.

[39]Walter Russell Mead has suggested that this is characteristic of the "Jacksonian" approach in U.S. politics: "Jacksonians believe that international life is and will remain both anarchic and violent. The United States must be vigilant and strongly armed. Our diplomacy must be cunning, forceful, and no more scrupulous than anybody else's. At times, we must fight pre-emptive wars. There is absolutely nothing wrong with subverting foreign governments or assassinating foreign leaders whose bad intentions are clear. Thus, Jacksonians are more likely to tax political leaders with a failure to employ vigorous measures than to worry about the niceties of international law." Walter Russell Mead, "The Jacksonian Tradition: And American Foreign Policy," The National Interest (Winter 1999–2000): 18.

CHAPTER 7

Conclusion

Do not bring me your historical Ph.Ds. Talk about the reality that this world is
in significant danger and that the only thing that can take us out of that danger
is when we develop the toughness to say that war is not an option.

Former U.S. Representative Ron Dellums

Israel will not die so that the world will speak well of it.

Golda Meir

Casting about for something that might be pressed into service as a
"threat," the Soviet Union's recent implosion having removed
that bogey from the horizon, the Joint Chiefs of Staff (JCS) nearly a
decade ago settled on "instability." Thus, they argued, "The threat is
instability and being unprepared to handle a crisis or war that no one
predicted or expected."[1] Democracy was in rising flower almost everywhere. In 1991–1992 twenty new members were admitted to the
United Nations, nearly all of which had some claim to democratic status. Because democracies don't threaten or fight democracies, as the
saying goes, one was obliged to look hard for adversaries. While North
Korea, Iraq, and Iran were singled out as "threats for which we must
maintain forces," clearly they would not suffice to underwrite the kind
and level of military forces the JCS preferred to maintain, so "instability" was embraced.

Espousing instability as the threat exposed only one more of the
symptoms of the cancer that has been eating away at the U.S. security
structure in general, and the U.S. military in particular. The ideal was
close at hand: democracy flourishing, reason replacing less "enlightened"

---

[1]United States, Joint Chiefs of Staff, *National Military Strategy of the United States* (Washington,
D.C.: U.S. Government Printing Office, 1992), 4.

approaches to ordering the affairs of man, the use of military force becoming an anachronism suitable only for the benighted or deranged. Conflict leading to the force of arms would everywhere be displaced by the peaceful settlement of disputes. Progress would in all cases and in all places be irenically implemented. A visceral aversion to causing citizens to offer their lives for a cause overlay the hubris—the confidence that bloodshed, the use of force, would not only be unnecessary, but in most cases criminal. The echoes of Kellogg-Briand were unmistakable.

Increasing the quantity and quality of constraints on the use of force went hand in hand with the increasing destructiveness of war. "The West," suggested George Will, "almost preens about having become too exquisitely sensitive to use force against barbarism."[2] Given this vision, the intent by "civilized states" was to establish modus operandi and rules to ensure that strong constraints on the use of force would be cemented in place, that there would be no backsliding, and that the road to "perpetual peace" would thereby be ensured.

The problem with all this is that it does not square with reality. It's a utopian vision, but subtly drawn—so much so that few fully appreciate it. Ralph Stacey looks at the issue through a clearer lens: "Today most of us are trying to explain a messy, opportunistic global competition game using mental models that focus on order, stability, cohesion, consistency, and equilibrium. . . . We do this because it is easier and more comfortable than feeling about in the dark for explanations that describe the world in terms of disorder, irregularity, unpredictability, and chance."[3] A little bit of idealism is healthy, but when it far exceeds the bounds of reasonableness, it must be reined in.[4]

Specifically, the vacuousness of instability as the threat was exposed by Paul Stockton, when he wrote—antedating its embrace by the Joint Chiefs—that "If stability is understood to mean only no war and a low probability of war and if this is made a prime national goal, then stabil-

---

[2]George F. Will, "Worthy of Contempt," *Washington Post*, August 3, 1995, 31.

[3]Ralph D. Stacey, *Managing the Unknowable: Strategic Boundaries between Order and Chaos in Organizations* (San Francisco: Jossey-Bass Publishers, 1992), 21.

[4]"Considering the disturbing history of international politics and the modern expansion of military power, all advocates of the restraint of force . . . must confess a degree of utopianism." Osgood and Tucker, *Force, Order, and Justice*, 192.

ity hamstrings action. It robs the nation of leverage in international affairs, making the use of power, either by violence, by threat, or by knowledge of the possibility that power will be used, impossible."[5]

One need not postulate a "clash of civilizations" to suggest that the world is not constituted solely of peace-loving democratic states and peoples. The world remains a disorderly place in which individual fanatics—not exclusively sovereign states—have gained access to weapons of mass destruction, and national power continues to be necessary to maintain the conditions in which freedom and justice might be possible. The reality is that national power still requires the ability to, when necessary, employ military force. Edward Luttwak argues that "[i]f the possessor of much of the world's military power refuses to use it, greater world disorder is only the most immediate consequence."[6] Indeed, the ability to use force is key to international order:

> Because it is the final arbiter of disputes and of conflicts of rights and interests which cannot be satisfactorily prevented, resolved, or redressed merely by inducements of law, reasoned persuasion, bargaining, and sympathy. It is the ultimate obstacle to the excesses of ambition and power that would otherwise destroy the balance of interests in a cohesive political system. It is the ultimate sanction behind the network of customs, laws, and procedures that enable a political system to operate routinely.[7]

Those charged with the responsibility for the actual application of force must, today, accept these facts:

- National security objectives will not be crystal clear, formulated in timely fashion, or fully underwritten by national will.

---

[5]Paul Stockton, "Strategic Stability between the Super-powers," *Adelphi Papers* 213 (Winter 1986): 90–91.

[6]Luttwak, "A Post-Heroic Military Policy," 44. Cf., "The most troubling aspect of the Vance-Owen plan is that it seeks a peaceful solution to a violent conflict through diplomatic efforts that unilaterally and publicly abjure the use of military force to compel compliance. As a consequence, the stronger and more aggressive party—in this case the Serbs—benefits." Zbigniew Brzezinski, "Will Airdrops and Talk Soften Serbs?" *Washington Times*, February 25, 1993, G1.

[7]Osgood and Tucker, *Force, Order, and Justice*, 31.

- To the extent that national security objectives are vague and imprecise, military objectives and the strategy to attain them will necessarily be flawed.

- Future threats can materialize and mature very quickly.

- No weapon in the hands of adversaries will be considered unusable.

- Planning for conflict is not the same as conducting it—the real world can never be completely anticipated or modeled.

- Execution never matches the perfection of the plan, the game floor, or the exercise scenario.

- There are no "country A's" and "country B's"; all are characterized by living human beings in a discrete context, and context is fundamental to conflict.

- Information will never be sufficient, there will always be unknowns, and, unfortunately, even unknowable risks.

- Friction and the fog of war will inevitably be present. Luck and chance will bedevil all scenarios.

- Strategic, operational, and tactical surprise will be crucial factors.

- Leadership will not be perfect; mistakes will be made.

- The torpedoes might not work; technology might well not live up to its promises.

- The weather will not cooperate.

- The adversary will react in unfavorable and unanticipated—indeed, asymmetrical—ways: that is the essence of strategy; it is not solitaire.

Indeed, at the end of his tenure as Secretary of Defense, William Perry demonstrated his sensitivity to the issue: "I think the biggest challenge any Secretary of Defense faces," he stated in an interview, "involves the use of force and getting it right, knowing when to use it, how to use it, and maintaining the forces in a state of readiness so that if you're called upon to use force, they're prepared to go."[8] Nevertheless, on top of all these considerations, the trend has been to choose deliberately to levy

---

[8]"The Use of Force and Getting It Right: Interview with Dr. William J. Perry," U.S. Naval Institute *Proceedings* (May 1997): 31.

constraints on the use of force, emanating from four sources: operational, organizational, legal, and moral.

The thesis is not that warfare, or the use of military force on the international scene, cannot or should not be controlled. It is in substantial agreement with the advice of Michael Howard: "To control and limit the conduct of war is thus not inherently impossible; indeed without controls and limitations war cannot be conducted at all. The difficulty lies in introducing and maintaining controls and limits derived from criteria other than those inherent in sound strategy and the requirement for 'good order and military discipline.' "[9] The contention here is that premeditatedly, voluntarily, the United States has been accepting and undertaking constraints on its ability to employ the military instrument such that it has lost many degrees of freedom, provided vulnerabilities and asymmetrical opportunities to those who would not be so constrained, and as a result increased its risks and decreased its security. No single constraint can be isolated as the cause of the problem: the cumulative weight of all of them is what has become oppressive.

Constraints and limitations on the use of force have been abetted by the confusion about threats to national security and the differences between the conduct of war and the enforcement of domestic laws. The threat of cross-border invasion of the United States has been virtually nonexistent since the inception of the Republic. Weakness to the north, weakness to the south, fish to the east, and fish to the west: that is what the United States has relied upon as its first line of defense.[10] It also has encouraged recurring seizures of isolationism. When the threat of weapons of mass destruction was coupled with intercontinental delivery systems, it was neutralized by the doctrine of mutual assured destruction. Yet, all components of this vision were passive. They suggested that national security can be ensured by a minimum investment and very little or no application of force. The absence of a sense of threat has been a strong contributor to the attractiveness of a growing menu of constraints on the use of force. "In those

---

[9]Howard, "Temperamenta Belli," in Howard, *Restraints on War*, 4.

[10]"The witty Jules Jusserand, French ambassador in Washington from 1902 to 1925, once quipped that America was blessed among the nations. On the north, she had a weak neighbor; on the south, another weak neighbor; on the east, fish; and on the west, fish." Thomas A. Bailey, *A Diplomatic History of the American People*, 6th ed. (New York: Appleton-Century-Crofts, Inc., 1958), 4.

Western liberal democratic countries," writes Josef Joffe, "where there is a very strong sense of threat . . . there is much less of a decline in the acceptability of force."[11]

Because of the burgeoning increase in constraints on the use of force, endemic in the West but most prevalent in the United States, both deterrence of undesirable acts and responses to them have been deeply undermined. The four axes of constraint analyzed here have created a fixed, lucrative target for potential enemies to exploit by what has come to be termed "asymmetrical means." The signals have been sent and received that the United States

- has scant interest in using force in a preventive fashion to forestall actions inimical to its security;
- must be deeply offended or wounded in order to respond;
- will respond only in fully legitimate, carefully measured, and scrupulously proportionate ways; and
- will restore damage and compensate "victims" of its forceful actions.

That is, the United States has virtually assured potential adversaries that it will respond to their actions only in particular, well-defined, reactionary, and very controlled ways.

Deterrence, however, is a full-time calling. It does not sleep, and malevolents are alert to these proclivities. Deterrence is not passive, a concept to be revisited periodically or when crises arise. The goal is not to avoid war but to prevent it.[12] Deterrence is truly a situation requiring eternal vigilance.

The trends, however, have been to confine and constrain the use or potential use of the military instrument, thereby tilting the battlespace unfavorably against the United States. "It is the rogue polity that sets the terms of engagement, not peaceable, satisfied polities," remarks Colin Gray, and that should, but has not, raised the alarum. Perhaps

---

[11]Joffe, "Democracy and Deterrence," in Miller and Smith, *Ideas and Ideals*, 115.

[12]Edward Luttwak offers a reminder in this regard that "no participant may choose to leave the game. He may turn his back; he may even proclaim his principled opposition to playing the game; but he must still pay his dues at each round, and the refusal to play merely means that he can lose but not win." *Strategy and Politics* (New Brunswick, N.J.: Transaction Books, 1980), 169.

"everything changed" on September 11, 2001; but the conduct of the campaign in Afghanistan and the initial confusion about how to deal with "battlefield detainees" and John Walker Lindh demonstrate that not everything has changed, and the confusion between warfare and law enforcement has not been clarified.

The use of force has increasingly been viewed as too expensive and too ineffective.[13] Yet, the contention of this book is that the use of force has become so constrained only through the deliberate actions of U.S. policy makers. The United States takes the constraints, much as it takes college students, too seriously. The United States has, without malice aforethought, backed unwittingly into the situation where it resembles mighty Gulliver, cinched down by Lilliputian strings. Self-imposed constraints have offered a rich breeding ground for asymmetrical actions by those free of such burdens. For the United States in its current composition—very strong militarily but with a willingness to use it that is heavily circumscribed—it might be rightly averred that the flesh is willing but the spirit is weak.[14]

Truly, it is a great dilemma because it reveals a shortcoming in understanding of the relationship between ends, ways, means, and risks. It also betrays a lack of interest in who wins. The ultimate logical result of ever-increasing constraints on the use of force is a consistent pacifism. One of the central characteristics of pacifism must be an indifference to who wins—to ends. To balance ends, ways, means, and risks, however, is the true challenge. Viewed in this way, pacifism is a cop-out.[15]

In order to balance these vital inputs to policy and strategy, to restore deterrence, and to level the battlespace against asymmetrical acts, U.S. policy makers will, first of all, have to acknowledge that there is a problem. Then the remedy will suggest itself. Carefully, a process

---

[13]Handel, War, Strategy, and Intelligence, 497.

[14]Stanley Hoffman has described the situation as "the great dilemma of Western society." "The more force is wrapped in political calculations and restraints . . . the less the [democratic] citizenry understands or approves of its use—this is surely the great dilemma of Western society in the final years of the 20th century." Quoted in Joffe, "Democracy and Deterrence," in Miller and Smith, Ideas and Ideals, 117.

[15]"Protestant theologian Reinhold Neibuhr insisted that Christians must look at the worldly impact of aggression and be prepared to counter it; pacifism is a form of Christian heresy, for it requires the Christian to stand impotent in the face of evil." Michael G. Roskin, National Interest: From Abstraction to Strategy (Carlisle, Pa.: Strategic Studies Institute, U.S. Army War College, 1994), 9.

should be initiated to understand and then to draft firm guidelines for the use of force. This should be viewed as a dynamic, living approach to working—not solving—the problem. The conditions that call for the use of force should be carefully worked out, and a system of alerts and responses prepared and implemented. This system would be under constant review and revision, but would consist of solid core requirements and less solid transient requirements. The core requirements would be subject to issuance of focused deterrence statements. The transient requirements might depend on general deterrence, or they might be the subject of their own focused deterrence pronouncements.

Constraints on the use of force should be reviewed in a holistic way. Where the impact of a particular constraint is evaluated as unnecessary or unnecessarily confining, it should be rolled back. The military instrument, in a messy, disorderly world, must be given freedom of action to accomplish the objectives assigned to it without either the assumption of unnecessary risks or providing opportunities for asymmetrical initiatives. Once again, the United States must renew its interest in who will prevail:

> For three decades, we have generally pursued, with the best of intentions and the best strategic analysis, a strategy for the use of conventional force that deviates sharply from earlier strategic traditions. It has emphasized not how to use force to win but how to avoid or to limit the use of force. In the nuclear age, these latter are clearly critical objectives, but they cannot be the only ones. The question we must ask is: What does the nature of American society and of earlier American strategic traditions tell us about how Americans can use force successfully?[16]

This cannot be done without the exertion of great amounts of effort, and it will necessarily be repugnant to those who distrust military options and those who choose and exercise them. When the defensive use of force, however, is clearly called for, U.S. decision makers and practitioners of the employment of military force must be granted at least a level field of operations and the ability to reduce the risks that must be run.

---

[16]Huntington, "Playing to Win," 14.

Select Bibliography

Adams, James. *The Next World War: Computers Are the Weapons and the Front Line Is Everywhere.* New York: Simon & Schuster, 1998.

Adams, R. J. Q., ed. *British Appeasement and the Origins of World War II.* Lexington, Mass.: D.C. Heath, 1994.

Aftergood, Steven. "The Soft-Kill Fallacy." *The Bulletin of the Atomic Scientists* (September/October 1994): 40–45.

Alberts, David S., and Daniel S. Papp, eds. *The Information Age: An Anthology on Its Impact and Consequences.* Washington, D.C.: The Center for Advanced Concepts and Technologies, 1997.

Albright, David. "South Africa and the Affordable Bomb." *Bulletin of the Atomic Scientists* 50, 4. Lexis Nexis, Dayton, Ohio: Lexis Nexis, June 13, 1996.

Arkes, Hadley. *First Things: An Inquiry into the First Principles of Morals and Justice.* Princeton, N.J.: Princeton University Press, 1986.

Arkin, William M., Damian Durrant, and Marianne Cherni. *On Impact: Modern Warfare and the Environment. A Case Study of the Gulf War.* London: Greenpeace, May 1991.

The Arms Control Reporter. Brookline, Mass.: Institute for Defense and Disarmament Studies, 1991.

Arquilla, John. *Dubious Battles: Aggression, Defeat, and the International System.* Washington, D.C.: Crane Russak, 1992.

————. "Strategic Implications of Information Dominance." *Strategic Review* (Summer 1994): 24–30.

Aspen Strategy Group. *The United States and the Use of Force in the Post-Cold War Era.* Queenstown, Md.: The Aspen Institute, 1995.

Axinn, Sidney. *A Moral Military.* Philadelphia: Temple University Press, 1989.

Bacevich, Andrew J. "Policing Utopia: The Military Imperatives of Globalization." *The National Interest* (Summer 1999): 5–13.

Bailey, Sydney Dawson. *Prohibitions and Restraints in War.* London: Oxford University Press, 1972.

————. *War and Conscience in the Nuclear Age.* New York: St. Martin's Press, 1987.

Bailey, Thomas A. *A Diplomatic History of the American People.* 6th ed. New York: Appleton-Century-Crofts, Inc., 1958.

Barnett, Jeffery R. *Future War: An Assessment of Aerospace Campaigns in 2010*. Maxwell AFB, Ala.: Air University Press, January 1996.

Barnett, Roger W. "Information Operations, Deterrence, and the Use of Force." *Naval War College Review* 51, 2 (Spring 1998): 7–19.

Bassiouni, M. Cherif. *Crimes against Humanity in International Criminal Law*. Dordrecht: M. Nijhoff Publishers, 1992.

Bennendijk, Hans, and Patrick Clawson. "Rethinking Grand Strategy." *The Washington Quarterly* 18, 2 (Spring 1995) [Electronic version].

Bennett, Bruce W., Christopher P. Twomey, and Gregory F. Treverton. *What Are Asymmetric Strategies?* Santa Monica, Calif.: RAND, 1999.

Bernstein, Richard. *Dictatorship of Virtue: Multiculturalism, and the Battle for America's Future*. New York: A. A. Knopf, 1994.

Best, Geoffrey. *War and Law since 1945*. Oxford: Clarendon Press, 1994.

Betts, Richard K. *Conflict after the Cold War: Arguments on Causes of War and Peace*. Boston: Allyn and Bacon, 1994.

———. *Surprise Attack: Lessons for Defense Planning*. Washington, D.C.: The Brookings Institution, 1982.

———. "The Delusion of Impartial Intervention." *Foreign Affairs*, November/December 1994, 20–33.

Blaker, James R. *United States Overseas Basing: An Anatomy of the Dilemma*. New York: Praeger, 1990.

Blank, Stephen J. *Conflict, Culture, and History: Regional Dimensions*. Maxwell Air Force Base, Ala.: Air War College, Air University Press, 1993.

Blechman, Barry M., William J. Durch, David R. Graham, John H. Henshaw, Pamela L. Rich, Victor A. Utgoff, and Steven A. Wolfe. *The American Military in the Twenty-First Century*. New York: St. Martin's Press in association with the Henry L. Stimson Center, 1993.

Blechman, Barry, and Cathleen S. Fisher. "Phase Out the Bomb." *Foreign Policy* 97 (Winter 1994–1995): 79–95.

Bueno de Mesquita, Bruce. *War and Reason: Domestic and International Imperatives*. New Haven, Conn.: Yale University Press, 1992.

Bull, Hedley. *The Anarchical Society*. London: Macmillan Press, 1977.

Bundy, McGeorge. *Danger and Survival: Choices about the Bomb in the First Fifty Years*. New York: Random House, 1988.

Butler, George Lee. *Statement at the National Press Club Newsmaker Luncheon, December 4, 1996*. Electronic Transcript. Washington, D.C.: Federal News Service, December 4, 1996.

Butts, Kent Hughes. *Environmental Security: What Is DOD's Role?* Carlisle Barracks, Pa.: Strategic Studies Institute, U.S. Army War College, 1993.

Byers, Michael. *Custom, Power, and the Power of Rules: International Relations and Customary International Law*. Cambridge: Cambridge University Press, 1999.

Campen, Alan D., and Douglas H. Dearth, contributing eds. *Cyberwar 2.0: Myths, Mysteries, and Reality.* Fairfax, Va.: AFCEA International Press, 1998.

Candland, Christopher. *The Spirit of Violence: An Interdisciplinary Bibliography of Religion and Violence.* New York: Harry Frank Guggenheim Foundation, 1992.

Carr, Edward Hallett. *The Twenty Years' Crisis, 1919–1939.* New York: Harper & Row, Harper Torchbooks, 1939.

Carus, W. Seth. *The Poor Man's Atomic Bomb? Biological Weapons in the Middle East.* Policy Papers, no. 23. Washington, D.C.: The Washington Institute for Near East Policy, 1991.

Charters, David D., J. Brent Wilson, and Marc Milner, eds. *Military History and the Military Profession.* Westport, Conn.: Praeger, 1992.

Clark, Ramsey, et al. *War Crimes: A Report on United States War Crimes against Iraq.* Washington, D.C.: Maisonneuve Press, 1992.

Clark, Robert D., Andrew M. Egeland, Jr., and David B. Sanford. *The War Powers Resolution.* A National War College Strategic Study. Washington, D.C.: National Defense University, 1985.

Clausewitz, Carl von. *On War.* Ed. and trans. Michael Howard and Peter Paret. Princeton, N.J.: Princeton University Press, 1976.

Cohen, Eliot A. "The Mystique of U.S. Air Power." *Foreign Affairs,* January/February 1994, 109–124.

———. "Three Comments." *The National Interest* (Winter 1993–94): 37–38.

Coll, Alberto R., James S. Ord, and Stephen A. Rose. *Legal and Moral Constraints on Low-Intensity Conflict,* International Law Studies 1995. Vol. 67. Newport, R.I.: Naval War College, 1995.

Conetta, Carl, and Charles Knight. *Dueling with Uncertainty: The New Logic of American Military Planning.* Cambridge, Mass.: Project on Defense Alternatives, Commonwealth Institute, February 1998. <http://www.comw.org/pda/bullyweb.html> (Accessed April 17, 1998).

Conversino, Mark J. "Sawdust Superpower: Perceptions of U.S. Casualty Tolerance in the Post-Gulf War Era." *Strategic Review* (Winter 1997): 15–23.

Cooke, Blanche Weisen, Sandi E. Cooper, and Charles Chatfield, eds. *Arbitration or War? Contemporary Reactions to the Hague Peace Conference of 1899.* New York: Garland Publishing, Inc., 1972.

Council on Foreign Relations. *Non-Lethal Technologies: Military Options and Implications.* Report of an Independent Task Force. New York: Council on Foreign Relations, 1995.

Crane, Conrad C. *Bombs, Cities, and Civilians: American Airpower Strategy in World War II.* Lawrence: University of Kansas Press, 1993.

Creveld, Martin Van. "The Persian Gulf Crisis of 1990–91 and the Future of Morally Constrained War." *Parameters* 22, 2 (Summer 1992): 21–40.

————. *The Transformation of War.* New York: The Free Press, 1991.

Cromartie, Michael, ed. *Might and Right after the Cold War: Can Foreign Policy Be Moral?* Washington, D.C.: Ethics and Public Policy Center, 1993.

Crovitz, Gordon, and Jeremy A. Rabkin, eds. *The Fettered Presidency: Legal Constraints on the Executive Branch.* Washington, D.C.: American Enterprise Institute for Public Policy Research, 1989.

Damrosch, Lori Fisler, and David J. Scheffer, eds. *Law and Force in the New International Order.* Boulder, Colo.: Westview Press, 1991.

Davis, Grady Scott. *Warcraft and the Fragility of Virtue: An Essay in Aristotelian Ethics.* Moscow: University of Idaho Press, 1992.

Davis, Malcolm. "How to Win Wars without Actually Killing." *Asia-Pacific Defense Reporter* (April–May 1994): 36–37.

De Atkine, Norvell B., and Daniel Pipes. "Middle Eastern Studies: What Went Wrong?" *Academic Questions* 9, 1 (Winter 1995–1996).

Demarest, Geoffrey. "The Strategic Implications of Operational Law." Ft. Leavenworth, Kans.: Foreign Military Studies Office, April 1995. <http://call.army.mil/fmso/fmsopubs/issues/oplaw.htm> (Accessed March 15, 1997).

DeSutter, Paula. "Deterring Iranian NBC Use." *Strategic Forum #110.* Washington, D.C.: National Defense University, April 1997. <http://call.army.mil/fmso/fmsopubs/issues/oplaw.htm> (Accessed May 12, 1997).

Dinstein, Yoram. *War, Aggression, and Self Defense,* 2nd ed. Cambridge: Grotius Publications, Cambridge University Press, 1994.

Dobkowski, Michael N. *Genocide in Our Time: An Annotated Bibliography with Analytical Introductions.* Ann Arbor, Mich.: Pierian Press, 1992.

Dunlap, Charles. "The End of Innocence: Rethinking Noncombatancy in the Post-Kosovo Era." *Strategic Review* (Summer 2000): 9–17.

————. *Technology and the Twenty-First-Century Battlefield: Recomplicating Moral Life for the Statesman and the Soldier.* Carlisle, Pa.: U.S. Army War College, January 15, 1999.

Earle, Edward Mead, ed. *Makers of Modern Strategy.* Princeton, N.J.: Princeton University Press, 1943.

Ederington, L. Benjamin, and Michael J. Mazarr, eds. *Turning Point: The Gulf War and U.S. Military Strategy.* Boulder, Colo.: Westview Press, 1994.

Ederly, Donald, and Michael Sherroden, eds. *The Moral Equivalent of War? A Study of Non-Military Service in Nine Nations.* New York: Greenwood Press, 1990.

Enthoven, Alain C., and K. Wayne Smith. *How Much Is Enough? Shaping the Defense Program, 1961–1969.* New York: Harper and Row, 1971.

Epstein, Joshua. "Horizontal Escalation: Sour Notes of a Recurrent Theme." *International Security* 8 (Winter 1983–1984): 19–31.

Erickson, Richard J. *Legitimate Use of Military Force against State Sponsored International Terrorism.* Maxwell Air Force Base, Ala.: Air University Press, 1989.

Evinger, William R., ed. *Directory of U.S. Military Bases Worldwide*. Phoenix, Ariz.: Oryx Press, 1995.

Franck, Thomas M. *Political Questions/Judicial Answers: Does the Rule of Law Apply to Foreign Affairs?* Princeton, N.J.: Princeton University Press, 1992.

Freedman, Lawrence, and Efraim Karsh. *The Gulf Conflict 1990–1991: Diplomacy and War in the New World Order*. Princeton, N.J.: Princeton University Press, 1993.

Fuller, Graham E., and Ian O. Lesser. "Persian Gulf Myths." *Foreign Affairs*, May/June 1997, 42–52.

Fussell, Paul. *Thank God for the Atom Bomb and Other Essays*. New York: Summit Books, 1988.

Gacek, Christopher M. *The Logic of Force: The Dilemma of Limited War in American Foreign Policy*. New York: Columbia University Press, 1994.

Gaddis, John Lewis. *The Long Peace: Inquiries into the History of the Cold War*. New York: Oxford University Press, 1987.

Galdorisi, George. "It's Time to Sign On." *United States Naval Institute Proceedings* (January 1998): 51–53.

Gardner, Richard. "International Law and the Use of Force, Paper II." *Adelphi Paper* no. 266. London: IISS, Winter 1991–1992.

Gauthier, Kathryn L. *China As Peer Competitor? Trends in Nuclear Weapons, Space, and Information Warfare*. Air War College Maxwell Paper, no. 18. Maxwell Air Force Base, Ala.: Air War College, July 1999.

Glahn, Gerhard von. *The Occupation of Enemy Territory*. Minneapolis: University of Minnesota Press, 1957.

Glynn, Patrick. "The Age of Balkanization." *Commentary*, July 1993, 21–24.

———. "Quantum Leap." *The National Interest* (Spring 1995): 50–57.

———. "The Sarajevo Fallacy—The Historical and Intellectual Origins of Arms Control Theology." *The National Interest* (Fall 1987): 3–32.

Goldstein, Judith, and Robert O. Keohane, eds. *Ideas and Foreign Policy: Beliefs, Institutions, and Political Change*. Ithaca, N.Y.: Cornell University Press, 1993.

Gong, G. W. *The Standard of "Civilization" in International Society*. Oxford: Clarendon Press, 1984.

Goulding, Vincent J., Jr. "Back to the Future with Asymmetric Warfare." *Parameters* (Winter 2000–2001): 21–30.

Gray, Colin S. "The Definitions and Assumptions of Deterrence: Questions of Theory and Practice." *The Journal of Strategic Studies* 13, 4 (December 1990).

———. *House of Cards: Why Arms Control Must Fail*. Ithaca, N.Y.: Cornell University Press, 1992.

———. *Weapons Don't Make War: Policy, Strategy, and Military Technology*. Lawrence: University Press of Kansas, 1993.

Greenberg Research, Inc. *The People on War Report.* ICRC Worldwide Consultation on the Rules of War. Geneva: International Committee of the Red Cross, October 1999.

Griffin, Susan. *A Chorus of Stones: The Private Life of War.* New York: Anchor Books, 1993.

Gutman, Roy, and David Rieff, eds. *Crimes of War: What the Public Should Know.* New York: W.W. Norton & Company, 1999.

Haass, Richard N. "Military Force: A User's Guide." *Foreign Policy* 96 (Fall 1994): 21–37.

Haber, L. F. *The Poisonous Cloud: Chemical Warfare in the First World War.* Oxford: Clarendon Press, 1986.

Halle, Louis J. *The Elements of International Strategy: A Primer for the Nuclear Age.* Vol. 10. Lanham, Md.: University Press of America, 1984.

Hammond, Grant T. "Paradoxes of War." *Joint Force Quarterly* (Spring 1994): 7–16.

———. *Plowshares into Swords: Arms Races in International Politics, 1840–1991.* Columbia: University of South Carolina Press, 1993.

Handel, Michael. *War, Strategy, and Intelligence.* London: Frank Cass, 1989.

Hannum, Hurst, ed. *Guide to International Human Rights Practice.* 2nd ed. Philadelphia: University of Pennsylvania Press, 1992.

Hansen, David G. *Militarism and Foreign Conflict Behavior: A Quantitative Study Revisited.* Carlisle Barracks, Pa.: U.S. Army War College, 1982.

Hanson, Victor Davis. "Sherman's War." *American Heritage,* November 1999, 58–66.

Harries, Owen. "American Power—For What: A Symposium." *Commentary,* January 2000. <http://ebird.dtic.mil/Jan2000/s20000105.concat.htm> (Accessed January 5, 2000).

Harris, Philip R. *Managing Cultural Differences.* 3rd ed. Houston, Tex.: Gulf Publishing Company, 1991.

Hayes, Bradd C. *Toward a Doctrine of Constraint.* Strategic Research Department Strategic Memorandum, no. 9-94. Newport, R.I.: Naval War College, 1994.

Hedrick, Larry. *Rogues' Gallery: America's Foes from George III to Saddam Hussein.* New York: Brassey's (U.S.), 1992.

Hemleben, S. J. *Plans for World Peace through Six Centuries.* New York: Garland Publishers, 1972 (1943).

Henkin, Louis, Stanley Hoffman, Jeane J. Kirkpatrick and Allen Gerson, William D. Rogers, and David J. Scheffer. *Right v. Might: International Law and the Use of Force.* 2nd ed. New York: Council on Foreign Relations Press, 1991.

Henry, Ryan, and C. Edward Peartree. *The Information Revolution and International Security.* Washington, D.C.: The CSIS Press, 1998.

Holt, Pat M. *The War Powers Resolution: The Role of Congress in U.S. Armed Intervention*. Washington, D.C.: American Enterprise Institute for Public Policy Research, 1978.

Howard, Michael. *Restraints on War: Studies in the Limitation of Armed Conflict*. Oxford: Oxford University Press, 1979.

Howard, Michael, and John F. Guilmartin, Jr. *Two Historians in Technology and War*. Carlisle Barracks, Pa.: U.S. Army War College, July 20, 1994.

Human Rights Watch. *Needless Deaths in the Gulf War: Civilian Casualties during the Air Campaign and Violations of the Laws of War*, A Middle East Watch Report. New York: Human Rights Watch, 1991.

Humphries, John G. "Operations Law and the Rules of Engagement." *Airpower Journal* (Fall 1992): 25–41.

Huntington, Samuel P. "Conventional Deterrence and Conventional Retaliation in Europe." *International Security* 8, 3 (Winter 1983–1984): 32–56.

———. "New Contingencies, Old Roles." *Joint Force Quarterly* (Autumn 1993): 38–43.

———. "Playing to Win." *The National Interest* (Spring 1986): 8–16.

Hyland, William G., and Charles William Maynes. *The Nature of the Post-Cold War World: Reexamining National Strategy*. Carlisle Barracks, Pa.: Strategic Studies Institute, U.S. Army War College, 1993.

Ikle, Fred C. "The Next Lenin: On the Cusp of Truly Revolutionary Warfare." *The National Interest* (Spring 1997): 9–19.

International Court of Justice. *Legality of the Threat or Use of Nuclear Weapons*. Advisory Opinion, July 8, 1996 (Paragraph 96). <http://disarm.ige.org/dticjtext.html> (Accessed April 13, 1997).

Iyengar, Shanto, and William J. McGuire, eds. *Explorations in Political Psychology*. Durham, N.C.: Duke University Press, 1993.

Jablonsky, David. *Time's Cycle and National Military Strategy: The Case for Continuity in a Time of Change*. Carlisle Barracks, Pa.: U.S. Army War College, June 1, 1995.

Johnson, James Turner. "The Broken Tradition." *The National Interest* (Fall 1996). 27–36.

Kagan, Donald. *On the Origins of War and the Preservation of Peace*. New York: Doubleday, 1995.

Kahn, Herman. *On Thermonuclear War*. Princeton, N.J.: Princeton University Press, 1960.

Kalshoven, Frits. *Constraints on the Waging of War*. International Committee of the Red Cross. Dordrecht, The Netherlands: Martinus Nijhoff Publishers, 1987.

Kanter, Arnold, and Linton F. Brooks, eds. *U.S. Intervention Policy for the Post-Cold War World: New Challenges and New Responses*. New York: W. W. Norton & Company, 1994.

Kaplan, Morton A., ed. *Strategic Thinking and Its Moral Implications.* Chicago: The University of Chicago Center for Policy Study, 1973.

Kaysen, Carl, Robert S. McNamara, and George W. Rathjens. "Nuclear Weapons after the Cold War." *Foreign Affairs,* Fall 1991, 95–110.

Keeva, Steven. "Lawyers in the War Room." *ABA Journal* 77 (December 1991). LEXIS-NEXIS. Dayton, Ohio: February 22, 1997.

Kroger, Daniel Paul. "Revolutionary Warfare and the Just War Tradition." Ph.D. diss. Ann Arbor, Mich.: University Microfilms International, 1992.

Kurzwell, Edith, and William Phillips, eds. *Our Country, Our Culture: The Politics of Political Correctness.* Boston: Partisan Review Press, 1994.

Lanier-Graham, Susan D. *The Ecology of War: Environmental Impacts of Weaponry and Warfare.* New York: Walker, 1993.

Lanman, Eric. "Wither the Warrior?" *United States Naval Institute Proceedings* (April 1998): 26–29.

Laqueur, Walter. "The West in Retreat." *Commentary,* August 1975, 44–52.

———. *The Political Psychology of Appeasement: Finlandization and Other Unpopular Essays.* New Brunswick, N.J.: Transaction Books, 1980.

Ledeen, Michael. "American Power—For What: A Symposium." *Commentary* (January 2000).

Lee, Steven. *Morality, Prudence, and Nuclear Weapons.* Cambridge: Cambridge University Press, 1993.

Leebart, Derek, ed. *Soviet Military Thinking.* London: George Allen & Unwin, 1981.

Legro, Jeffrey. "Cooperation within Conflict: Submarines, Strategic Bombing, Chemical Warfare and Restraint in World War II." Ph.D. diss. Ann Arbor, Mich.: University Microfilms International, 1993.

Leonard, James E. *Chemical Warfare: An Urgent Need for a Credible Deterrent.* Carlisle Barracks, Pa.: U.S. Army War College, 1982.

Levie, Howard S. *Terrorism in War: The Law of War Crimes.* Dobbs Ferry, N.Y.: Oceana Publications, 1993.

Liang, Qiao, and Wang Xiangsui. *Unrestricted Warfare.* FBIS Translation. Beijing: PLA Literature and Arts Publishing House, 1999.

Liotta, P. H. "A Strategy of Chaos." *Strategic Review* (Spring 1998): 19–29.

Lomov, N. A., ed. *Scientific Technical Progress and the Revolution in Military Affairs.* Trans. and publ. under the auspices of the U.S. Air Force. Washington, D.C.: U.S. Government Printing Office, 1974.

Lowe, Vaughan, and Colin Warbrick. *The United Nations and the Principles of International Law.* London: Routledge, 1994.

Luttwak, Edward N. "A Post-Heroic Military Policy." *Foreign Affairs,* July/August 1996, 33–44.

———. "Toward Post-Heroic Warfare." *Foreign Affairs,* May/June 1995, 109–122.

————. *Strategy and Politics*. New Brunswick, N.J.: Transaction Books, 1980.

Lyons, David. *Moral Aspects of Legal Theory: Essays on Law, Justice and Political Responsibility*. Cambridge: Cambridge University Press, 1993.

MacCrimmon, Kenneth R., and Donald A. Wehrung, with W. T. Stanbury. *Taking Risks: The Management of Uncertainty*. New York: The Free Press, 1986.

McCall, Sherman. "A Higher Form of Killing." *United States Naval Institute Proceedings* (February 1995): 40–45.

McCoubrey, H. *International Law and Armed Conflict*. Aldershot, Hants; Brookfield, Vt.: Dartmouth, 1992.

McElroy, Robert W. *Morality and American Foreign Policy: The Role of Ethics in International Affairs*. Princeton, N.J.: Princeton University Press, 1992.

McKenzie, Kenneth F., Jr. *The Revenge of the Melians: Asymmetric Threats and the Next QDR*. McNair Paper no. 62. Washington, D.C.: National Defense University, 2000.

McMillan, Joseph. "Talking to the Enemy: Negotiations in Wartime." *Comparative Strategy* 11, 4 (October/December 1992): 447–461.

McNamara, Robert S. *The Essence of Security: Reflections in Office*. New York: Harper and Row, 1968.

————. "The Military Role of Nuclear Weapons: Perceptions and Misperceptions." *Foreign Affairs*, Fall 1983, 59–80.

Mandelbaum, Michael. "A Perfect Failure." *Foreign Affairs*, September/October 1999 [Electronic version].

Mann, Paul. "Pentagon Called Unprepared for 'Post-Modern' Conflict." *Aviation Week and Space Technology*, April 27, 1998, 54–56.

Mann, Steven R. "Chaos Theory and Strategic Thought." *Parameters* (Autumn 1992): 54–68.

Maoz, Zeev. *Paradoxes of War: On the Art of National Self-Entrapment*. Studies in International Conflict, Vol. 3. Boston: Unwin Hyman, 1990.

Matthews, Lloyd J., and Dale E. Brown, eds. *The Parameters of Military Ethics*. Washington, D.C.: Pergamon-Brassey's, 1989.

Mead, Walter Russell. "The Jacksonian Tradition: And American Foreign Policy." *The National Interest* (Winter 1999–2000): 5–29.

Meilinger, Phillip S. "Winged Defense: Airwar, the Law, and Morality." *Armed Forces and Society* 20, 1 (Fall 1993): 103–123.

Meinhold, Richard J. *Beyond the Sound of Cannon: Military Strategy in the 1990s*. Jefferson, N.C.: McFarland, 1992.

Metz, Steven, and Douglas V. Johnson II. *Asymmetry and U.S. Military Strategy: Definition, Background and Strategic Concepts*. Carlisle Barracks, Pa.: Strategic Studies Institute, U.S. Army War College, January 2001.

Miall, Hugh. *The Peacemakers: Peaceful Settlement of Disputes since 1945*. New York: St. Martin's Press, 1994.

Miles, Franklin B. *Asymmetric Warfare: An Historical Perspective*. Carlisle Barracks, Pa.: U.S. Army War College, 1999.

Miller, Linda B., and Michael Joseph Smith. *Ideas and Ideals: Essays on Politics in Honor of Stanley Hoffman*. Boulder, Colo.: Westview Press, 1993.

Moore, John Norton, Guy B. Roberts, and Robert F. Turner. *National Security Law Documents*. Durham, N.C.: Carolina Academic Press, 1995.

Mott, Commander C. P. "Naval Forces After . . . From the Sea." *United States Naval Institute Proceedings* (September 1993): 44–46.

Mueller, John, and Karl Mueller. "Sanctions of Mass Destruction." *Foreign Affairs*, May/June 1999: 49–53.

Mulinen, Frederic de. *Handbook on the Law of War for Armed Forces*. Geneva: International Committee of the Red Cross, 1987.

Munro, Neil. *The Quick and the Dead: Electronic Combat and Modern Warfare*. New York: St. Martin's Press, 1991.

Murphy, John Francis, and Bernard H. Oxman. *Nonviolent Responses to Violence-Prone Problems: The Cases of Disputed Maritime Claims and State-Sponsored Terrorism*. Reports of two special committees of the American Society of International Law. Washington, D.C.: The American Society of International Law, 1991.

Murray, Williamson. "The Meaning of World War II." *Joint Force Quarterly* (Summer 1995): 54–55.

Murray, Williamson, MacGregor Knox, and Alvin Bernstein. *The Making of Strategy: Rulers, States and War*. New York: Cambridge University Press, 1994.

Mylroie, Laurie. "The World Trade Center Bomb: "Who is Ramzi Yousef? And Why It Matters." *The National Interest* (Winter 1995–1996): 3–15.

National Academy of Sciences, Committee on Technology for Future Naval Forces. *Technology for the United States Navy and Marine Corps, 2000–2035: Becoming a Twenty-First-Century Force*. Washington, D.C.: National Academy of Sciences, 1997.

Newland, Samuel J., and Douglas V. Johnson II. "The Military and Operational Significance of the Weinberger Doctrine." *Small Wars and Insurgencies* 1, 2 (August 1990): 171–190.

Niebuhr, Reinhold. *Moral Man and Immoral Society: A Study in Ethics and Politics*. New York: Scribner, 1960.

Nitze, Paul H. "Deterring Our Deterrent." *Foreign Policy* 25 (Winter 1976–1977): 195–210.

Northedge, F. S., ed. *The Use of Force in International Relations*. New York: The Free Press, 1974.

Nuechterlein, Donald. *America Overcommitted*. Lexington, Ky.: University of Kentucky Press, 1985.

Nye, Joseph. "Home and Abroad." *The National Interest* (Fall 1996): 89–92.

Omega Foundation. *An Appraisal of the Technologies of Political Control.* An Omega Foundation Summary and Options Report for the European Parliament. September 1998. <http://cryptome.org/dst-1.htm> (Accessed August 11, 2000).

Osgood, Robert E., and Robert W. Tucker. *Force, Order, and Justice.* Baltimore, Md.: The Johns Hopkins University Press, 1967.

Pape, Robert A. *Bombing to Win: Air Power and Coercion in War.* Ithaca, N.Y.: Cornell University Press, 1996.

Paret, Peter. *Innovation and Reform in Warfare.* The Harmon Memorial Lectures in Military History, no. 8. Colorado Springs, Colo.: United States Air Force Academy, 1966.

Payne, James L. *The American Threat: The Fear of War as an Instrument of Foreign Policy.* Chicago: Markham Publishing Company, 1970.

Peters, Charles. "Tilting at Windmills." *Washington Monthly,* September 1995 [Electronic version].

Peters, Ralph. "The New Warrior Class." *Parameters* 24, 2 (Summer 1994): 16–26.

Petraeus, David H. "The American Military and the Lessons of Vietnam." Ph.D. diss. Ann Arbor: University of Michigan Microfilms, 1987.

———. "Military Influence and the Post-Vietnam Use of Force." *Armed Forces and Society* 15, 4 (Summer 1989): 489–507.

Phillips, Guy R. "Rules of Engagement: A Primer." *The Army Lawyer.* U.S. Department of the Army Pamphlet 27–50–248. July 1993: 4–27.

Pick, Daniel. *War Machine: The Rationalization of Slaughter in the Modern Age.* New Haven, Conn.: Yale University Press, 1993.

Pipes, Daniel. "There Are No Moderates: Dealing with Fundamentalist Islam." *The National Interest* (Fall 1995): 48–57.

Porter, Bruce D. *War and the Rise of the State: The Military Foundations of Modern Politics.* New York: Free Press, 1994.

Postman, Neil. *Technopoly: The Surrender of Culture to Technology.* New York: Vintage Books, 1993.

Prokosh, Eric. *The Technology of Killing: A Military and Political History of Antipersonnel Weapons.* London: Zed Books, 1995.

Quigley, John B. *The Ruses for War: American Interventionism since World War II.* Buffalo, N.Y.: Prometheus Books, 1992.

Record, Jeffrey. *Hollow Victory: A Contrary View of the Gulf War.* Washington, D.C.: Brassey's (U.S.), Inc., 1993.

———. *Perils of Reasoning by Historical Analogy: Munich, Vietnam, and American Use of Force since 1945.* Occasional Paper No. 4. Maxwell Air Force Base, Ala.: Air University, March 1998.

Regan, Geoffrey. *The Book of Military Blunders.* Santa Barbara, Calif.: ABC-CLIO, 1991.

Reid, Brian Holden, ed. *The Science of War: Back to First Principles*. London: Routledge, 1993.

Roberts, Adam. "International Law and the Use of Force, Paper I." *Adelphi Paper*, no. 266. London: IISS, Winter 1991–1992.

Robertson, Horace B., Jr. "Contemporary International Law: Relevant to Today's World?" *Naval War College Review* (Summer 1992): 89–103.

Rodman, Peter W. "American Power—For What: A Symposium." *Commentary*, January 2000. <http://ebird.dtic.mil/Jan2000/s20000105.concat.htm> (Accessed January 5, 2000).

Romm, Joseph J. *Defining National Security: The Nonmilitary Aspects*. New York: Council on Foreign Relations Press, 1993.

Rosenberg, Barbara. " 'Non-lethal' Weapons May Violate Treaties." *The Bulletin of the Atomic Scientists* (September/October 1994): 44–45.

Roskin, Michael G. *National Interest: From Abstraction to Strategy*. Carlisle, Pa.: Strategic Studies Institute, U.S. Army War College, 1994.

Ross, Bruce. "The Case for Targeting Leadership in War." *Naval War College Review* (Winter 93): 73–93.

Rothgeb, John M. *Defining Power: Influence and Force in the Contemporary International System*. New York: St. Martin's Press, 1993.

Rummel, R. J. *Death by Government*. New Brunswick, N.J.: Transaction Publishers, 1994.

———. "Political Systems, Violence, and War." *Command* 38, 1 (Spring 1989).

Russell, F. H. *The Just War in the Middle Ages*. London: Cambridge University Press, 1975.

Russett, Bruce M. *Controlling the Sword: The Democratic Governance of National Security*. Cambridge, Mass.: Harvard University Press, 1990.

———. *Grasping the Democratic Peace: Principles for a Post-Cold War World*. Princeton, N.J.: Princeton University Press, 1993.

Ryan, Michael E. "Washington Watch: Lessons Learned and Re-Learned." *Air Force Magazine*, August 1999.

Sarkesian, Sam C., and John Mead Flanagan, eds. *U.S. Domestic and National Security Agendas into the Twenty-first Century*. Westport, Conn.: Greenwood Press, 1994.

Schelling, Thomas. "What Went Wrong with Arms Control?" *Foreign Affairs*, Winter 1985–1986, 219–233.

Schlesinger, Arthur, Jr. "The Necessary Amorality of Foreign Affairs." *Harper's Magazine*, August 1971, 72–77.

Schmitt, Major Michael N. "The Resort to Force in International Law: Reflections on Positivist and Contextual Approaches." *Air Force Law Review* 37, 105 (1994): 105–120.

Schneider, Barry R., and Lawrence E. Grinter, eds. *Battlespace of the Future: Twenty-First-Century Warfare Issues.* Air War College Studies in National Security No. 3. Maxwell Air Force Base, Ala.: Air University Press, September 1995.

Schwarz, Benjamin C. *Casualties, Public Opinion, and U.S. Military Intervention: Implications of U.S. Regional Deterrence Stategies.* Santa Monica, Calif.: RAND, 1994.

Seabury, Paul, and Angelo Codevilla. *War: Ends and Means.* New York: Basic Books, Inc., Publishers, 1989.

Shrader, Charles R. *Amicicide: The Problem of Friendly Fire in Modern War.* Combat Studies Institute Research Survey No. 1. Ft. Leavenworth, Kans.: U.S. Army Command and General Staff College, 1982.

Shue, Henry, ed. *Nuclear Deterrence and Moral Restraint: Critical Choices for American Strategy.* Cambridge: Cambridge University Press, 1989.

Shultz, Richard H., Jr. *In the Aftermath of War.* Maxwell Air Force Base, Ala.: Air University Press, 1993.

Simpson, Christopher. *Science of Coercion: Communication Research and Psychological Warfare, 1945–1960.* New York: Oxford University Press, 1994.

Sloan, Stanley R. *The United States and the Use of Force in the Post-Cold War World: Toward Self-Deterrence?* Washington, D. C.: U.S. Government Printing Office, 1994.

Smock, David R. *Religious Perspectives on War: Christian, Muslim, and Jewish Attitudes toward Force after the Gulf War.* Washington, D.C.: United States Institute of Peace Press, 1992.

Snider, Don M. "America's Postmodern Military." *World Policy Journal* (Spring 2000) [Electronic version].

Sommers, Christina Hoff, and Frederick Tamler Sommers. *Vice and Virtue in Everyday Life: Introductory Readings in Ethics.* 3rd ed. Fort Worth, Tex.: Harcourt Brace Jovanovich College Publishers, 1993.

Spykman, Nicholas J. *America's Strategy in World Politics: The United States and the Balance of Power.* Hamden, Conn.: Archon, 1970 (1942).

Stacey, Ralph D. *Managing the Unknowable: Strategic Boundaries between Order and Chaos in Organizations.* San Francisco: Jossey-Bass Publishers, 1992.

Stanton, Martin N. "Nonlethal Weapons: Can of Worms." *United States Naval Institute Proceedings* (November 1996): 59–60.

———. "What Price Sticky Foam?" *United States Naval Institute Proceedings* (January 1996): 58–60.

Stavridis, James. "The Second Revolution." *Joint Force Quarterly* (Spring 1997): 8–13.

Steel, Ronald. *Temptations of a Superpower.* Cambridge, Mass.: Harvard University Press, 1995.

Stern, Gary M., and Morton H. Halperin, eds. *The U.S. Constitution and the Power to Go to War: Historical and Current Perspectives.* Westport, Conn.: Greenwood Press, 1994.

Stockton, Paul. "Strategic Stability between the Super-powers." *Adelphi Papers,* no. 213 (Winter 1986).

Summers, Harry G. *On Strategy II: A Critical Analysis of the Gulf War.* New York: Dell, 1992.

Szafransky, Richard. "Peer Competitors, the RMA, and New Concepts: Some Questions." *Naval War College Review* 49, 2 (Spring 1996): 113–119.

Thompson, Kenneth W. *Traditions and Values in Politics and Diplomacy: Theory and Practice.* Baton Rouge, La.: Louisiana State University Press, 1992.

Timmerman, Frederick W. Jr. "Future Warriors." *Military Review* (September 1987): 46–55.

Tirpak, John A. "The State of Precision Engagement." *Air Force Magazine,* March 2000 [Electronic version].

Toner, James Hugh. *True Faith and Allegiance: The Burden of Military Ethics.* Lexington: University Press of Kentucky, 1995.

Tucker, Jonathan B. "Asymmetric Warfare." *Forum for Applied Research and Public Policy* (Summer 1999) <http://forum.ra.utk.edu/specialreport.html> (Accessed September 17, 2000).

Turner, Robert F. *Repealing the War Powers Resolution: Restoring the Rule of Law in U.S. Foreign Policy.* Washington, D.C.: Brassey's (U.S.) Inc., 1991.

Turney-High, Harry Holbert. *Primitive War, Its Practice and Concepts.* Columbia: University of South Carolina Press, 1971.

United Nations. *Peaceful Settlement of Disputes between States: A Selective Bibliography.* New York: United Nations, 1991.

U.S. Arms Control and Disarmament Agency. *Parties and Signatories of the Biological Weapons Convention.* November 4, 1996. Electronic Document, <http://www.acda.gov/treaties/bwcsig.txt> (Accessed March 31, 1997).

———. *Threat Control through Arms Control.* Report to Congress, 1994. Washington, D.C.: U.S. Arms Control and Disarmament Agency, 1995.

United States. Congress. House. Committee on Armed Services. *The Use of Force in the Post-Cold War Era: Hearings,* March 3 and 4, 1993. Washington, D.C.: U.S. G.P.O., 1993.

United States. Department of the Air Force. *International Law—The Conduct of Armed Conflict and Air Operations.* AFP 110–31. Washington, D.C.: Department of the Air Force, November 19, 1976.

———. *An Introduction to Air Force Targeting.* AFT 200–17. June 23, 1989.

United States. Department of the Army. *Operations.* Field manual 100–5. (FM 100–5) June 1993.

United States. Department of Defense. *Report of the Secretary of Defense on the FY66–70 Defense Program*. Washington, D.C.: U.S. Government Printing Office, 1965.

———. *Report of the Secretary of Defense on the FY68–72 Defense Program*. Washington, D.C.: U.S. Government Printing Office, 1967.

———. *Report of the Secretary of Defense on the FY69–73 Defense Program*. Washington, D.C.: U.S. Government Printing Office, 1968.

———. *Annual Report of the Secretary of Defense, Fiscal Year 1987*. Washington, D.C.: U.S. Government Printing Office, 1988.

United States. Department of the Navy. Office of the Chief of Naval Operations. *The Commander's Handbook on the Law of Naval Operations*. NWP 1–14M. Revised 10/01/1998. Newport, R.I.: Naval War College, 1998.

———. Chief of Naval Operations, Strategic Studies Group XVI. *Naval Warfare Innovation Concept Team Reports*. Newport, R.I.: Naval War College, Strategic Studies Group, June 1996.

United States. Federal Bureau of Investigation, Counterterrorism Threat Assessment and Warning Unit, National Security Division. *Terrorism in the United States 1998*. Washington, D.C.: 1998.

United States. Joint Chiefs of Staff. Chairman of the Joint Chiefs of Staff Instruction (TI) 3121.01, *Standing Rules of Engagement for U.S. Forces* (U), October 1, 1994.

———. *Concept for Future Joint Operations*. Washington, D.C.: U.S. Government Printing Office, 1997.

———. *Joint Vision 2010*. Washington, D.C.: U.S. Government Printing Office, 1996.

———. *Joint Vision 2020*. Washington, D.C.: U.S. Government Printing Office, 2000.

———. *National Military Strategy of the United States*. Washington, D.C.: U.S. Government Printing Office, January 1992.

United States. National Defense University, Institute for National Strategic Studies, *Strategic Assessment 1998*. Washington, D.C.: National Defense University, 1998. <http://www.ndu.edu/inss/sa98?sa98ch11.html> (Accessed October 2, 2000).

United States. Office of the Secretary of Defense. *Conduct of the Persian Gulf Conflict: An Interim Report to Congress*. Washington, D.C.: U.S. Government Printing Office, July 1991.

United States. President. *A National Security Strategy for a New Century*, <http://www.whitehouse.gov/WH/EOP/NSC/Strategy/, May 1997> (Accessed September 15, 1997).

U.S. Physicians for Human Rights. *Landmines: A Deadly Legacy*. New York: Human Rights Watch, 1993.

Wakin, Malham M., ed. *War, Morality, and the Military Profession*. 2nd ed. Boulder, Colo.: Westview Press, 1986.

Warbrick, Colin, Vaughan Lowe, and Michael Barton Akehurst. *The United Nations and the Principles of International Law: Essays in Memory of Michael Akehurst*. London: Routledge, 1994.

Warren, Spencer. "Churchill's Realism: Reflections on the Fulton Speech." *The National Interest* (Winter 1995): 38–49.

Warschaw, Tessa Albert. *Winning by Negotiation*. New York: McGraw-Hill, 1987 (1980).

Weart, Spencer. "Why They Don't Fight: Democracies, Oligarchies, and Peace." *In Brief*, no. 48. Washington, D.C.: United States Institute of Peace, November 1993.

Webb, R. C., Les Palkuti, Lew Cohn, Glenn Kweder, and Al Constantine. "The Commercial and Military Satellite Survivability Crisis." *Defense Electronics*, August 1995, 21–25.

Weigley, Russell F. *The American Way of War: A History of United States Military Strategy and Policy*. New York: Macmillan, 1973.

Weir, William. *Fatal Victories*. Hamden, Conn.: Archon Books, 1993.

Weiseltier, Leon. "When Deterrence Fails." *Foreign Affairs*, Spring 1985, 827–847.

Weston, Burns H., and Richard Pierre Claude. *Human Rights in the World Community: Issues and Action*. 2nd ed. Philadelphia: University of Pennsylvania Press, 1992.

White, Rodney. *North, South, and the Environmental Crisis*. Toronto: University of Toronto Press, 1993.

Wohlstetter, Albert J. *Legends of the Strategic Arms Race*. Washington, D.C.: U.S. Strategic Institute, 1975.

Wood, Robert S. "Strategic Choices, Geopolitics, and Resource Constraints." *The Washington Quarterly*, Summer 1989 [Electronic version, LEXIS-NEXIS (Accessed October 15, 2001)].

Wright, Quincy. *A Study of War*. Abridged. Chicago: University of Chicago Press, 1964.

Zakheim, Dov. "Preparing for a World to Unravel." *ROA National Security Report*, August 1995.

Zumwalt, James G. "The 'Law of War'—Bringing Civility to the Battlefield." *Marine Corps Gazette*, February 1995, 45–47.

Index

About the Author

Roger W. Barnett, Ph.D., is an award-winning author and professor emeritus at the U.S. Naval War College in Newport, Rhode Island. A retired U.S. Navy captain, he held a variety of posts while on active duty, including the command of a guided-missile destroyer, and was head of both the Strategic Concepts Branch and the Extended Planning Branch in the Office of the Chief of Naval Operations. He has published numerous essays, articles, and reviews on naval affairs, national military strategy, arms control, and security policy. With Colin S. Gray, he coedited *Seapower and Strategy*, published by the Naval Institute Press in 1989. He lives in Newport, Rhode Island.